Beginning in the Nursery Business

Third Edition
Newly Revised and Expanded

By
John J. Pinney
Robert D. Pinney, Ph.D.

COPYRIGHT ©1985 BY
AMERICAN NURSERYMAN
PUBLISHING CO. INC.

All rights reserved. No part of this book may be reproduced or transmitted in any form or by any means, electronic or mechanical, including photocopying, recording or by any information storage and retrieval system, without permission in writing from the Publisher.

AMERICAN NURSERYMAN PUBLISHING
  CO. INC.
111 NORTH CANAL STREET
CHICAGO, IL 60606

Printed in the United States of America

CONTENTS

	Page
1. Introduction	1
2. Garden Centers	12
3. Landscape Nurseries	22
4. Agency Nurseries	31
5. Mail-Order Nurseries	33
6. Container-Grown Nursery Stock	44
7. Interior Landscaping	49
8. Wholesale Nurseries	53
9. Financing and Records	62
10. Miscellany	66

FOREWORD

After World War II, the nursery industry experienced many changes. Previously, nursery stock was field-grown in rows like corn. Today, a high percentage of it is produced in containers. Originally, the major portion of nursery stock was sold to consumers by door-to-door salesmen and by catalogs issued by mail-order companies. The catalogs are still with us, but the salesmen have almost completely disappeared. In their place, we have garden center operators and landscape nurserymen, who cater to all the needs of gardeners and homeowners. These changes, all for the better, amount to a revolution in the industry.

This book attempts to describe the nursery industry as it is conducted today. It does not explain how to operate a nursery; rather, it tries to provide enough information to help readers decide whether the nursery business is an industry they would like to enter.

About the Authors

John J. Pinney is a retired nurseryman with more than 50 years experience in the business.

Robert D. Pinney, John's son, grew up in the nursery business. He received a doctoral degree in plant pathology from the University of Wisconsin, Madison.

Chapter 1. Introduction

Introduction

So you are thinking about going into the nursery business. If you decide that operating a nursery is the career for you, you will be welcomed into one of the most fascinating businesses in the world. It is never monotonous, never cut and dried; every day brings different satisfactions and pleasures.

The nursery business is the division of agriculture comprising the growing of trees, shrubs, flowers, fruits and vegetables. In practice, these activities are separated into four categories. Flower growers are called florists; fruit growers are pomologists; vegetable growers are olericulturists; and growers of trees and shrubs are nurserymen.

Working with plants is a constant challenge. There are new varieties to study, new uses to learn and new markets to develop. The appearances and performances of plants cannot be standardized. Nurserymen must become familiar with their individual ways.

A nursery business is one that gives its owner endless satisfaction. It is forever producing health-giving fruit, life-renewing gardens and breathtaking landscpes. It brings beauty to rich and poor, young and old alike. As the owner of a nursery business, you should never be ashamed but always proud. You will be associated with a fine group of sincere people, who are often leaders in their communities, always respected citizens. A person who loves trees and plants cannot be bad at heart.

The nurseryman's wares are among the few commodities that increase in value and give customers more satisfaction as years go by. You can justly believe that you are rendering a necessary and important service when you increase the fruitfulness and beauty of the good earth. Nursery products contribute to man's spiritual welfare as well as to his material comfort.

Although there are no records of nurseries existing in ancient times, there must have been plantsmen skilled in propagating plants. In the fourth century B.C., Theophrastus, a Greek, compiled a list of plants suitable as food, medicine or both. A similar list was drawn up in the first century A.D. by Dioscorides, a Greek army doctor and the "father of botany." His list has survived and served as an authoritative reference for many centuries. It is logical to assume that there were ways to propagate these plants so they could be used.

The Romans used thousands of roses in their festivals. Their avenues were lined with trees. These plants must have been produced in nurseries.

Growing plants commercially was an established practice by the 17th century. The first nursery in North America was started by William Prince in 1750 in Flushing, NY, on Long Island. It survived the Revolution and counted George Washington and Thomas Jefferson among its customers.

Nurseries in the US began to proliferate early in the 19th century. As early as 1840, hundreds of thousands of fruit trees were being grown by US nurserymen. Today, thousands of nurseries, both wholesale and retail, are operating. And the industry continues to enjoy a healthy growth.

The Future is Bright

What is the future of the nursery business? Leaders in the industry believe that the opportunities for nurserymen are greater now than at any time in the past. They have several reasons for their optimism.

The US population is increasing rapidly. Millions of new homes will have to be built to house new families. It is a safe bet that most new homes will be landscaped. Nearly every home builder now realizes that the job is not complete until the grounds have been planted.

Many years of research and observation prove that plantings of trees and

BEGINNING IN THE NURSERY BUSINESS

shrubs play an important role in conserving energy, an area of concern in the future. Windbreaks and screen plantings can cut heating costs by reducing wind velocity. They can also increase summer comfort with their shade. Tree and shrub screen plantings blot out undesirable views and greatly reduce traffic and other noises. They also significantly improve the quality of the air and are very useful in controlling soil erosion.

A comparatively new market for nursery stock is industrial landscaping. Instead of permitting their grounds to grow to weeds or look like junkyards, industries are now making their factories and warehouses as attractive as possible, both inside and out. Employees are happier and more efficient in pleasant surroundings. Thousands of new factories will have to be built to supply the growing demand for consumer goods, expanding this new market.

People are constantly searching for ways to reduce air pollution. Trees have a definite place in this battle. The filtering effect of their foliage has been demonstrated, and their life processes add much-needed oxygen to the atmosphere. Tree planting is bound to increase as the battle intensifies.

Perhaps most important of all is the fact that the US is coming of age. As the country matures, more people appreciate beauty. When a nation is new, its people's energies are spent in developing its resources or struggling to make a living. With increasing leisure and wealth, people try to surround themselves with luxury and beauty.

The Eastern Seaboard of this country, for example, is a better market for ornamental nursery stock than are many newer areas. Taste and appreciation have been developed to a higher degree. Now that the frontiers have disappeared and communities are growing older, homeowners yearn for more pleasant surroundings.

Incomes are increasing, and work weeks are shorter; nearly everyone has more leisure time and money. Many people who formerly had no interest in gardening have discovered that working with growing things can be a fascinating hobby. Gardening has become one of America's foremost hobbies and is likely to remain so.

Disadvantages

But we would be remiss if we did not tell you about some of the nursery business's disadvantages, which are not immediately apparent to outsiders. The nursery trade is seasonal. Therefore, income is irregular. Careful financing is necessary to carry on during the lean months.

Although B&B trees and container-grown materials can be planted anytime the ground can be worked, the public is not geared to year-round planting. Most is still done in spring and fall.

It is not practical to maintain office and field crews large enough for peak periods during the slack seasons. Therefore, when orders are being filled during the rush seasons, everyone has to work long hours under pressure. Extra employees are needed.

This disadvantage of annual humps and hollows is one of the hardest to overcome. The best brains in the industry are trying to determine how to level the humps and fill in the hollows to make the business more uniform year-round. Progress is being made. Using containers to grow and market nursery stock is proving a great boon to the industry.

Like all other forms of agriculture, horticulture is subject to the whims of weather. Unseasonable weather may cut short the planting season or cause heavy losses of trees and shrubs already planted. Hail, snow, sleet, frost, flood or drought may bring calamity. Only a few of these risks can be insured. No amount of foresight or

INTRODUCTION

planning can circumvent such setbacks.

Do not expect to get rich quickly or amass a big fortune in the nursery business. Few indeed are the people who have done so. Successful nurserymen can expect, however, to make good livings, maintain their families in comfort and give their children good educations.

If you have not already chosen the community in which you wish to locate, you can gain a great initial advantage by carefully considering several important factors. In general, large cities are better suited to cash-and-carry businesses. The more homeowners, the more potential customers a nursery has. Avoid cities top-heavy with apartments or rented homes. Be sure there is not too much local competition.

For example, a highly profitable retail nursery business was developed in a few years in a city of fewer than 75,000 people. It was a city of fairly wealthy homeowners that lacked a progressive retail nursery to take care of the demand in that field.

The nurseryman (we will call him Green) established the business with no previous experience in the business other than some success in growing roses in his own backyard. His neighbors admired his rose garden and wanted him to supply them with rosebushes like his. So he began selling on commission for the company from which he had bought his roses.

Sensing the possibilities in the field, Green selected a site near the edge of a good, rapidly developing residential area which had room for expansion and no zoning restrictions against a nursery. On this site, he built an attractive combination home, office and salesroom. Consistent advertising in newspapers and on local channels brought Green a satisfactory volume of cash-and-carry business.

The city was growing rapidly. Many new homes were being built, and there was no one in the community to landscape them. Green had many calls for landscape services he did not feel qualified to render. However, with the encouragement of his wholesale nurseries and the assistance of qualified men in these companies, he was soon supplying plans and doing landscape plantings.

With experience came confidence. In a few years, Green was drawing and executing his own plans and had developed a profitable landscape service in addition to his cash-and-carry business. The point we wish to emphasize is that Green had chosen the right community in which to establish his business. It was comparatively easy for him because he had a large potential market and no serious competition.

It may seem that such communities are rare, but any wholesale nurseryman can give you the names of many towns and cities that are excellent potential markets for nursery stock but in which there are either no nurseries or no wide-awake nurserymen offering serious competition.

The population of a city is not always a good criterion for judging the size of the market there. Some industrial cities, especially heavily manufacturing ones, are notoriously poor markets for nursery stock. Cities in which there are small yards or no yards at all or in which there is a high percentage of apartments or rented homes are also poor places to sell nursery stock. Choose a community where people live in their own homes and take pride in them.

Often a comparatively small city draws retail trade from many miles around. This is especially true in the Midwest and West, where many towns of only a few thousand people support a retail trade as great as that of other cities several times larger.

A good example of this is one Midwestern town of 6,000 people. An energetic young man decided to start a nursery there and to solicit trade from surrounding towns that had no nurseries. There were several within a short driving distance. He advertised regularly with the local radio station and newspaper, which both served wide areas. Before long, he had developed a prosperous business.

A recent trend in horticulture is to combine a nursery with a florist. This combination has always existed to some extent, but it is becoming more common today, especially in towns too small to support separate flower shops and nurseries.

In fact, this combination is to be encouraged because one business supplements the other. The nursery business in all but the extreme South is seasonal, while the florist business has fewer humps and hollows. The nurseryman who also operates a floral business not only enjoys steadier income but is also able to maintain a better year-round organization.

This practice of a dual business often confuses many customers. Because they do not distinguish between the two operations, they expect to buy flowers from a nurseryman and trees and shrubs from a florist.

If your capital is limited, you might do well to follow the example of many who have started in the nursery business. Choose the city or town in which you wish to locate and get a job that ensures you an income while you are establishing the business. If you already live in the town of your choice and have a job, so much the better. Look around for a suitable location. Take your time so that you do not make a mistake. Having secured what you want, plan carefully and in detail.

By working during your spare time, you can eventually get your business established. You might even be able to start operating it in your spare time; it has been done many times. When you think your business is on a firm foundation, you can quit your job and devote your full time to being a nurseryman.

Location of Your Nursery

Retail nurseries should be readily accessible. Locations on busy highways are not always best. Rapidly moving traffic resists all stops. Most of a retail nursery's business comes from local residents, not from transients.

The exact location of your nursery within a city is not easy to decide. Large mercantile organizations searching for good locations for their branch stores study every angle carefully. They analyze traffic movement and density, parking facilities and space requirements. The trend within the retail trade is away from congested downtown areas to suburban districts, which are nearer to homes and have more parking space.

Experience has shown that a nursery located near a rapidly developing residential area is better than one near or in an older area. Newer homes need landscaping. Their owners are young people who want to improve their surroundings as quickly as possible. Older, established areas are already well-planted. Their needs are mostly replacement.

Perhaps the best location for a nursery is on a highway not too far from the residential part of a city. It can be outside the city proper, on a high-traffic street in the city between the residential and business districts or actually in the residential district if there are no zoning restrictions. Try to choose a location where the most potential customers can see your place when traveling their usual routes. The farther customers have to go out of their way to reach you, the less likely you are to sell to them. Conversely, the more accessible your establishment is, the greater business volume you can expect.

It must be acknowledged, however, that there are notable exceptions. There are examples of successful retail nurseries located several miles from a

INTRODUCTION

city. By advertising extensively and offering inducements to visit, these nurseries have built up enviable businesses. Extreme examples can be cited. A nursery located 50 miles from a city of 1 million people has built up a profitable weekend trade by advertising in the city's major papers. Facilities are provided for the comfort of visitors from the city who treat the trip as a weekend outing.

If you decide to locate your business next to a highway, try to select a site on the outside of a curve. Your place will be spotted more readily, and motorists are traveling slowly, so they will be more likely to stop. Many new highways have limited access. This means that people can enter or leave the highways only at designated points, which are usually found at infrequent intervals. To reach adjoining property, motorists must follow service roads that run parallel to the highway. This is an inconvenience that discourages many customers.

Be sure that the zoning laws affecting your property allow you to operate a nursery business. Do not take the real estate agent's word; check with the appropriate officials. Sometimes you can arrange to have property that has been zoned for other purposes rezoned for business. But don't take a chance. Many people have bought properties with the owner or real estate agent's assurance that they could be rezoned to later find that they could not.

However, it is easier to have a property zoned for a nursery than for almost any other type of business. Residents usually have no prejudice against nurseries and are likely to think of them as assets. They visualize displays of attractive trees, shrubs and flowers.

In deciding how much ground you need for your nursery, be sure you have plenty of space for (1) off-street parking, (2) display ground, (3) buildings and (4) expansion.

You need off-street parking space and plenty of it. Your customers should be able to drive off the street onto your grounds and park without danger of being hemmed in by someone parking behind them. This requires a considerable amount of ground, especially if you are to do the volume of business you hope to do. Perhaps the most common error in planning a salesyard is not providing easily accessible and adequate parking space.

There is no rule to follow in determining the amount of land needed to establish a retail nursery business. Some successful nurseries operate from city lots. Others occupy several acres. It would be hard to set up a well-planned retail nursery with adequate facilities on less than one acre; a larger area would be better. Along a highway, a long, shallow strip is better than a deep one with a narrow frontage. You can design a more satisfactory layout with long frontage.

One highly successful garden center is located in a suburb's completely built-up downtown business section. It has only 17,500 square feet of space for display and storage. There is no parking lot, so customers must park on the street or in a public lot with meters. Despite these handicaps, this garden center has a very prosperous business.

Before you begin construction, make a complete plan on paper so you can study it carefully and try to dig out all the bugs. Unless you have had previous experience and know just about what you want, you would do well to visit as many nurseries as you can to get ideas. In this way, you can avoid costly errors; on the other hand, you will get suggestions that will help you start right.

Another thing you can do to help gather ideas is to talk to successful merchants in other retail businesses. After all, the principles of selling are similar for all lines of merchandise. Other retailers might be able to help you plan your displays.

Parking Cars

How many times have you failed to buy an article because you could not find a place to park near the store? Keeping this in mind, you should make parking simple and inviting. Put the parking area where it can be seen easily from the highway and is accessible. Arrange it so that the parking plan is obvious.

Cars parked helter-skelter reduce the parking space and increase the danger of accidents. Customers are not going to feel kindly toward you if other customers dent their fenders. Be sure that parked cars do not interfere in any way with the visibility and accesibility of your displays or with loading purchases into other cars.

It would be difficult to overemphasize the importance of providing adequate parking space for your customers' cars. This can best be illustrated by the experience of one Midwestern garden center. The site was near a rapidly developing residential suburb. The area set aside for parking was deemed adequate to accommodate all the cars that the business was likely to attract at any one time.

However, before the garden center operator realized that the lot was not large enough, all the surrounding ground was covered with new houses. Expansion was out of the question. Many customers now have to park on the street. When traffic is heavy, special policemen are needed to direct it.

When choosing a site for the parking lot, customer convenience is the first consideration. The best place for the lot is as near to headquarters as possible. Customers should not be required to walk long distances.

It is not necessary to spend a lot of money building an elaborate structure, especially when you are just getting started and are anxious to keep your expenditures to a minimum. But, by all means, make the buildings as attractive as possible, no matter how small they are. We have seen otherwise attractive nurseries spoiled by ugly, unpainted shacks serving as offices.

Even small buildings can be attractively designed. If you are clever at planning, you may be able to put up a small building that can be enlarged later without spoiling its architecture.

Do not fail to landscape your buildings. A well-kept lawn helps a lot. How often nurserymen fail to practice what they preach! You can make a mighty favorable impression on your customers by surrounding your buildings with a beautiful and dignified planting. It is your best advertisement.

Selecting Stock to Sell

The most critical job in establishing a nursery is deciding what to sell. Of what value are the most skillfully laid selling plans if you do not have what the public wants? One of the hardest lessons many nurserymen have to learn is that the most profitable nursery stock is not necessarily that which is easiest to grow or the kind they like best; rather, it is the kind the customers want.

Fortunately, you do not need to guess. Accurate, dependable information is available. Wholesale nurserymen know from experience just what varieties of fruit and ornamental stock are in demand in a given region. They also know in what proportions they can be expected to sell. Progressive wholesale nurserymen keep accurate records. Therefore, their recommendations are not a matter of guesswork or memory. Varieties that do not sell enough to be profitable are discarded from their assortments.

Regrettably, many varieties that have great merit have not proven popular enough to be profitable. In general, the best-known varieties are the ones that sell best. Everyone has heard of Elberta peaches. It is no trouble at all to sell Elberta peach trees through retail outlets; they are much easier to

INTRODUCTION

sell, in fact, than many other less familiar but better quality peach trees.

Give the public what it wants. If you keep that in mind when you select your starting stock, you cannot go far wrong. Your original investment should be almost entirely in varieties of known popularity. After you have started your business and established your clientele, you can add other varieties for which you have had a consistent demand. Remain alert to customer inquiries for varieties you do not have so that you will know what additional varieties it will pay to stock.

Where Should You Buy It?

Perhaps by this time you are wondering where you should buy your nursery stock. The following suggestions may prove helpful.

You are pretty safe if you buy stock from companies that advertise consistently in the nursery trade journals. Trade journals, especially those in the nursery industry, are very conscious of their responsibilities to their subscribers. They guard against irresponsible advertisers by carefully checking trade references. A nursery with a shady reputation would have a difficult time buying advertising space in a trade journal.

Most large wholesale nurseries today employ salesmen who are assigned territories. They call on the retail nurserymen in their areas, usually at roughly regular intervals. Many of these salesmen have worked in nurseries and are well-informed about the plants they have for sale. They know what plants sell best in their territories and can recommend new and meritorious plants.

Because these salesmen visit many nurseries, they gather great stores of valuable information about successful marketing and enlightened management. They are happy to pass their insights to their customers. Accordingly, retail nurserymen should welcome their visits, and listen to them. They can be very helpful.

Today, many wholesale catalogs are very informative. Not only do they illustrate many plants in full color, but they also provide succinct descriptions. They are an important aid in keeping retailers up to date on plant material.

By getting prices from many wholesale houses and distributing your orders widely, you may save small amounts on some items. But, in the long run, you will find that practice does not work out to your advantage. In the first place, you will have to keep track of many different purchases, thereby complicating your office work. Receiving stock in many small shipments not only increases delivery and packing costs but can also produce numerous inconveniences, such as failures to ship on time, delays in transit or errors in filling orders. You actually save money by confining your purchases to a comparatively few wholesalers.

Another advantage that we should emphasize is the reward for loyalty. If you buy from the same nurseries year after year, they will go all out to help you when the going gets rough. When stock is scarce, regular customers will be favored. Should you need extended credit, you will find your wholesale houses inclined to be lenient. Have confidence in your wholesale sources. Consult them frequently, and respect their advice.

Displaying nursery stock for sale presents several problems. Much of the stock is dormant and leafless when sales begin in spring. Bare branches are not at all attractive and offer no clues as to the plants' appearances when in leaf and bloom. Color pictures and descriptions are required to inform the customer.

When bare-root plants are offered for sale, they must be heeled in upright in beds or bins with moist packing material, such as sawdust or peat, around the roots. When bare-root trees and shrubs break dormancy and the leaves come out, they should no longer be sold because the risk of their dying is too high. Usually, when these plants remain unsold when they break dormancy, they must be discarded. This can result in substantial losses for a nurseryman.

Fortunately, great improvements have been made in the methods of preparing nursery stock for sale. Nurserymen no longer have to offer bare-root plants. For early season sales, when trees, shrubs and roses are still dormant, wholesale nurserymen can sell plants whose roots are packed in moisture-retaining material and wrapped in waterproof paper.

These packaged plants are identified by color picture labels. Many packages are very attractive. Furthermore, they keep the plants in good condition for a long time if they are displayed away from sun and wind.

Packaged plants usually go on sale very early in the season — at times it seems almost too early. However, unseasonably warm days always come along early in spring, and gardeners are tempted to buy. Dormant plants can be set out any time the ground can be worked. The availability of these packaged plants has extended the selling season.

Another great advance in marketing came when plants were first grown in containers. This practice began commercially in a small way about 50 years ago, chiefly on the West Coast. It has now spread to all parts of the country.

Plastic or metal containers with capacities of 1 to 15 gallons are most commonly used. Container-grown plants can be set out at any time during spring, summer or autumn, even when in full leaf and actively growing, until the ground freezes. Container-grown plants greatly extend the selling season for nursery stock. Sales can continue all summer into autumn.

It should not be assumed that container-grown stock has taken over the market. Field-grown plants still represent the major portion of marketable nursery stock. However, containers are gaining. Practically all fruit, shade and ornamental trees are field-grown. Many are planted into pots for convenient handling. Millions of rosebushes sold every year are all field-grown, and most of them are potted for retail sales.

Interestingly, growing plants in containers is a centuries-old practice. Pliny's "Historia Naturalis" (1513) has a woodcut showing a workman setting a plant into a basket. A German book of plants published in Strasbourg in 1518 includes an illustration of a woman watering a plant in a wooden tub.

Evergreens — spruces, pines, firs, junipers, yews and the like — are easy to display well. They are in full dress year-round. Field-grown evergreens are dug with balls of earth around their roots. Burlap is then placed around the ball to hold it in place. The trade calls this balled and burlaped, or B&B, material.

More container-grown evergreens are becoming available. Many of them are large enough for immediate effect in landscape plantings. One advantage pot-grown evergreens have over field-grown B&B evergreens is the ease with which they can be kept in good condition by watering. Earth balls do not readily absorb moisture. Therefore, they must be kept moist by placing packing material, such as peat or sawdust, around the balls.

Another common practice introduced a few years ago is transplanting field-grown plants into pots. This is commonly done with shrubs, small evergreens, fruit trees, small shade and ornamental trees and especially with roses. These transplants put out new roots and usually give better results than bare-root nursery stock. Individually potted plants can be displayed to

INTRODUCTION

their best advantage.

Allied Sales Lines

One of the big problems in all nursery businesses is managing finances between the main planting seasons. In most sections of the country, the heaviest sales of nursery stock are in spring. The next best season is fall. During the rest of the year, sales drop sharply. Retail nurserymen have an advantage in this respect because they can sell allied lines of merchandise during summer. Bedding plants, vegetable plants, seeds, insecticides, fertilizers and garden tools are some of the lines that can supplement plant sales.

These additional items bring more customers and increase your business volume. A customer who buys a bag of fertilizer is a potential buyer of a rose garden and vice versa.

There are some people who object to a nursery's offering anything but nursery stock. They are also opposed to drugstores selling sandwiches, tobacco shops selling hats and grocery stores selling aspirin. Customers have no such prejudices. If you can supply them with their needs, you will keep their interest. These shifts in retailing have come to stay, and more rearrangements are on the way.

Are you worried about selling nursery stock because you do not know much about it? That should not cause you much concern. Much more important are your personality, natural ability to sell and attitude toward the business. Some people are born salesmen. Many others acquire the art. The principles are the same for any kind of selling. We do not propose to present a course in salesmanship, but perhaps the following suggestions may guide you in the right direction.

There are many good books on salesmanship. A thoughtful reading of one or two should prove helpful. Observe the methods of any good salesman, especially those in retail establishments. The more you know about the products you are selling and their uses, the better prepared you are to sell them. You can pick up much information by reading descriptive nursery catalogs or, better still, by visiting large nurseries during their growing season.

Plant Knowledge

Technical knowledge of plants is not essential. We would much rather take a chance on hiring a person who knows nothing about nursery stock but has a pleasing personality and some sales ability than the most highly trained horticultural technician. This statement does not mean we believe that the less salesmen know about a product, the easier it is for them to sell it or that the technically trained person cannot sell. Quite the contrary: you cannot know too much about your product. But there is a big difference between technical information and the kind that interests the public.

For example, suppose a salesman told customers that the botanical name of flowering almond is Prunus glandulosa, that its branches are glabrous or slightly pubescent and that the leaves are broad elliptic to obovate. The customers probably would be duly impressed by the salesman's learning, but do you think this information would have created a desire to buy? Of course, this illustration is greatly overdrawn, but we have actually observed comparable examples.

On the other hand, customers might buy if they knew that flowering almond's flowers are like tiny, double, pink roses appearing in early spring before the leaves come out and in such large masses that the twigs are obscured. Customers would like to know that the shrub tolerates drought and heat and never grows too rank to get out of bounds.

As an example, one young man was hired as a salesman in a garden center. He was a graduate of a 4-year course in horticulture at a state university. He had specialized in plant material and was well-informed. However, when he described the merits of a plant, he talked at such great length and in such detail that customers became bored, and he made no sales.

Women who have a great love for plants often make excellent salesmen. Their enthusiasm is contagious. It is easy for them to sell because they know firsthand what pleasure growing things can bring. Like all fans, they are eager to share their fun with others. It is common practice to employ women in nurseries, one that has brought satisfactory results.

Landscape Principles Are Helpful

Some familiarity with the principles of landscape design is desirable in nursery salesmen. One way to acquire this knowledge is to study some of the many books on landscape gardening that have been written for laymen.

Most customers do not know precisely what they want when they visit your nursery. They may have some vague ideas, but usually they require some help before they make up their minds. They may prefer just to walk around for a while to see what you have and what appeals to them before they are ready to talk to you. Be tactful in such cases, and do not press for a sale until they show some signs of wanting to talk things over. Try to get them to outline their problems fully. Then you can make more intelligent suggestions and be more helpful. On the other hand, if customers know exactly what they want, never try to argue them out of it, unless it involves plants that are utterly unsuited for the purpose.

No method of selling makes as high a percentage of customers out of prospects or orders of inquiries as personal salesmanship. Keep this in mind at all times, and make the salesmen aware of it, too. When your prospect calls on you, you immediately gain a great advantage; do not muff it. No amount of newspaper advertising or direct mail follow-up is as effective as what you say and do when customers are in your store.

Ban High Pressure

Remember that using high-pressure methods to make a sale is worse than making no sale at all. The largest department store in the world gives its salespeople strict instruction not to use any pressure to make a sale. The management knows that the ill will caused by such methods more than offsets the profit from the sale. A prospect who fails to buy today may be back tomorrow if he is treated with so much courtesy and consideration that he knows he is welcome whether he comes to buy or only to browse.

If you want to test the truth of this statement, put yourself in the customer's place. The chances are you can think of some stores you never go into at all if you can avoid them because you are uncomfortable if you do not buy something.

Many of your visitors come out of curiosity or with only a half-formed notion of buying. These are the ones on whom you have to practice the art of salesmanship with all your skill. Your job is to arouse so strong a desire for your products that the prospect becomes a customer. To do this, you should be thoroughly familiar with the reasons it is desirable to buy nursery stock, the product's selling points.

Selling Points

Here are a few of the obvious selling points: No investment of equal cost increases the value of your property as much as nursery stock. Improvements consisting of nursery stock continue to grow in value year after year; all other improvements begin to deteriorate immediately. A well-landscaped home sells far more readily than one which has no planting at all. Homes, schools,

INTRODUCTION

offices and factories with beautiful surroundings make happier and more efficient occupants. It is fun to grow your own fruits and flowers and to sell or give away the surplus. There is a fascination with things that grow and a great satisfaction in helping them grow well.

Dense plantings of trees and shrubs are effective sound barriers, as well as substantial aids in reducing air pollution. In rural areas, both evergreen and deciduous trees are used extensively for windbreaks and shelterbelts.

Orchards and berry farms are still profitable investments if they are operated in a businesslike manner. Everyone enjoys the comfort of a shade tree on a hot summer day. Some people like to mark the boundaries of their property with hedges or screen plantings. Privacy can be gained by planting outdoor living rooms. Berry-bearing shrubs attract many songbirds.

No doubt other selling points will occur to you. Become thoroughly familiar with them so that you can bring them into casual conversations, thereby sowing the seed of an idea that may grow and flower into a sale.

Do not oversell. Sometimes it is easy to do, but it does not build goodwill. If you sell a customer 100 hedge plants when 75 are enough, he will soon find out. Often, perhaps more often than not, buyers do not really know how many plants they need and are not able to provide enough information for you to advise them correctly. In such cases, it is better to be conservative and point out that you would rather sell too few plants than too many. Tell customers that if they need more plants, they can come back for them later. Meanwhile, the plants will stay in better condition in your hands than in theirs.

Frequently when customers return, they think of something else that they want. In the long run, you sell more this way than if you oversell to customers the first time.

The nursery industry has undergone greater changes since World War II than during the 100 years before the war. Not only have these changes affected production but marketing procedures as well.

Chapter 2. Garden Centers

Garden Centers

A little history of the garden center industry may be of interest. Beginning before World War II and culminating after the war, almost a complete revolution of the chief method of marketing nursery stock occurred. Beginning way back in the early part of the past century, nursery stock was sold by salesmen (or agents, as they were usually called), who went door to door in town and country. For the most part, they were independent agents working on commission. The travelling salesman remained the principal way of marketing nursery stock until the Great Depression of the 1930s.

A number of nurseries had thousands of agents selling for them, creating a market for great quantities of nursery stock. But with the Depression, it became more and more difficult to sell nursery stock. Interestingly, fruit trees represented a very important part of the nursery trade at that time. Tree agents sought other employment, and sales fell so much that some large nurseries went out of business.

Mail-order nurseries had existed ever since the middle of the 19th century. Many were well-established and able to weather the Depression. Competition from tree salesmen no longer existed. So, many more mail-order nurseries were established until hundreds existed in the country.

During the time that tree agents were calling door to door, local retail nurseries were selling limited assortments of nursery stock. Usually, this stock was heeled in in the ground in rows or beds and dug as sales were made. If gardeners needed spades or hoes, they went to a hardware store. A drugstore was their source for chemicals to control insects and diseases. About the only mulches available were bales of straw or hay purchased at a feed store.

Astute nurserymen began to stock such related items. An idea that home gardeners should be able to get all their needs in one place grew. From this idea came the concept of the garden center. By the end of World War II, it was firmly established.

Some companies were already being referred to as garden centers. However, the term was first applied to centers set up in certain cities, including Denver and Cleveland. Their purpose was to serve as a source of gardening information. They usually had libraries and demonstration gardens. For a time, there was confusion about just what a garden center was, but the term is now universally applied to full-service local nurseries.

The garden center industry originated in the US and soon spread to other countries. Great Britain quickly adopted the concept and, in many ways, improved upon it. Today, garden centers are found in most European countries, Australia and New Zealand. There is an international organization of garden centers. And garden centers account for most nursery stock sales to consumers.

Much of what we have already said about retail nurseries applies also to garden centers. However, some of those suggestions need elaboration, because garden centers are much more complicated operations, requiring greater investment.

A garden center's location is important. If your only source of income is to be the cash-and-carry trade attracted by a garden center, you should locate on a well-traveled road in an area that has a dense population of homeowners. A lot of traffic is necessary to build a profitable cash-and-carry trade. On the other hand, if you plan to operate your garden center along with a landscape business, you can be successful in smaller communities.

A shopping center is an ideal place in which to establish a garden center. The traffic it creates should attract many potential customers, and there is usually ample parking space.

But the disadvantages of locating in a shopping center often outweigh the advantages. Rents are high. And there is usually little space for displaying nursery stock. At times, it is not possible to park nearby. So customers (or you) have to carry purchases considerable distances. This poses a real problem with very heavy or bulky items, such as large, balled evergreens or bales of peat. Nevertheless, there are numerous examples of successful garden centers in shopping centers.

Communities with a high percentage of homeowners and without any established nurseries are ideal locations for garden centers. There are many cities without nurseries or garden centers that would welcome such enterprises.

After you have decided on your community, choose your exact location with care. The "going-home" side of a through street or trafficway serving a residential area is the ideal spot, provided the traffic is not too fast. However, garden centers located on side streets are also often successful.

Properties located close to a population center on streets carrying heavy traffic often become so high-priced that nurserymen cannot afford to use them for their businesses. Taxes might also be prohibitive. It is important to keep the initial investment as modest as possible, while meeting the necessary requirements for a garden center. It is better to locate farther from town on less expensive land and to create traffic by advertising.

Be sure that the land on which you plan to establish your business is zoned for that type of operation. Check with county or city officials. Sometimes it is possible to have the land rezoned to suit the business, but you should be certain of this before you invest. Neighbors, even in residential areas, seldom object to a well-run nursery. Be sure that adequate water and sewer facilities are available.

A common mistake in establishing garden centers is building them on sites that are too small. Perhaps the most important consideration is providing ample and easily accessible parking space. A long, narrow strip along a highway is better than a deeper strip with only a short frontage.

It should be easy for customers to drive into your place of business and find a place to park. Try to arrange the parking in such a way that it is clear where and how customers should park. Use small, neat signs if necessary. The parking area should be covered with gravel or an all-weather surface. A common error is to place the parking lot too far from the main building. Customers should not have to walk far to reach the area where they can get service.

Before you begin to build your garden center, make a detailed, scaled plan on paper. List all of the features you want to incorporate, and relate them to each other. You need a building for your salesroom and office. Most garden centers have lath or shade houses, and many have small conservatories or greenhouses where they display and sell bedding plants, vegetables and houseplants.

In all planning, customer convenience should have prime consideration. Customers should not have to hunt for parking places. Loading purchases into their cars should be easy and convenient.

The arrangement of your garden center deserves careful study.

Lay the parking lot parallel to the street or highway to make access easy. Place your buildings parallel to the long axis of the parking lot, so they present their greatest dimensions to the street. This results in a more impressive appearance to passers-by while proving more convenient for customers. Such a layout allows customers to see your entire establishment at a glance and makes it easier to visit the parts that interest them most.

Give much thought to the garden shop's design. There has been a trend to design buildings with unique, far-out designs. Their purpose is to attract attention. They may serve this purpose, but there is a danger of going too far. One such garden shop comes to mind. The front was unique but attractive. When customers approached the building from the street, the entrance was not obvious. They might walk to one end only to discover that the door is at the other.

The arrangement of the buildings is also important. They should be placed so that additions can be built without disturbing any of the standing structures. For example, if a garden shop is placed so there is plenty of open space at both ends and behind it, a greenhouse could be built at one end and a shade house at the other. Then, if more room is needed in the shop, it can be added in the rear. Additions could also be made easily to both the greenhouse and shade house. There should be easy access directly from the store to these structures.

One design that is becoming popular consists of a central, unroofed patio with a shade house, garden shop, conservatory and other facilities built around it. This offers an attractive layout without sacrificing convenience. The patio is used for attractive displays of merchandise that do not need protection from the weather. Statuary, fountains, lawn furniture, barbecues and plants that need no shade are good possibilities for this area. Umbrella-covered lawn tables and chairs can give customers a place to relax, observe the surrounding merchandise and perhaps enjoy cold drinks or coffee.

Another modern trend is to turn the whole garden center into a garden, making all the merchandise a part of the design. Instead of displaying plants in rows in beds, such garden centers incorporate them into an overall design, giving customers the impression that they are walking through a big garden. All components are connected by a walk that goes all the way through the grounds. Garden centers that have adopted this plan are enjoying immense popularity.

It is not necessary to spend excessive money on your garden center. The prime considerations are roominess, convenient arrangement and neatness. No building is inexpensive these days, but buildings constructed at comparatively low cost can be attractive as well as functional. Elaborate salesrooms with expensive looks may discourage many customers who think your prices will also be high. Strive for an attractive design but one that is not extreme. You might find it pays to employ an architect. Architects can create pleasing designs as well as keep construction costs down.

A word of caution is timely. An architect who has no knowledge of the nursery business or the needs of a garden center operator might design a building that is attractive but impractical. It has happened a number of times. If you employ an architect, work with him and insist on a building design that is attractive and practical.

Give Yourself Enough Room

A common error in planning sales buildings is to make them too small. You will need adequate room to properly display your merchandise, and you should provide some space for your office. If possible, put your office somewhere that is not too accessible to the public. You need privacy to get your work done. Usually, the rest rooms are placed in the sales or store building. If cost is a limiting factor, the building can be made smaller at first but should be designed so that it can be enlarged without damaging the overall plan.

Because the salesroom or store building is the heart of your garden center, it should be in a prominent spot

GARDEN CENTERS

where it will be recognized readily and reached easily. The requirements usually mean it will be the central feature of the store's layout.

One common practice has been to have large windows across the front of a garden shop, but they reduce the amount of valuable wall space that is needed for display. Many garden centers are now built without large windows. They depend on artificial lighting. Painting the interior walls and ceilings bright colors helps to create a cheerful atmosphere.

Garden centers can be set up without lath or shade houses. Many centers in the Northern states have cool summers and manage to get along without any shade. But in the south, some shade is desirable. Aside from the value of shade to plants, there is a psychological factor involved in displaying plants under shade. It not only improves the plants' appearances but it also weakens the customers' sales resistance. One large garden center that was doing a good business without shade decided to build a small lath house to protect its shade-loving plants. The result was a marked increase in plant sales. Now nearly all of this garden center's nursery stock is displayed under shade.

The shade house should be near the salesroom and, if possible, attached to it. This arrangement is convenient for customers. Lay the shade house out with its greatest dimension parallel to the street and, if possible, construct it as an extension of the salesroom. This creates a long, impressive structure, and all parts are easily accessible. The front of the shade house should be open, permitting customers to enter from any point in the parking lot.

Many shade houses are now constructed of steel posts with lightweight steel girders supporting the lath. They are attractive and long-lasting but costly. If you wish to build a less expensive structure, you can use 2- or 3-inch used iron pipe set in concrete on 10- or 12-foot centers. Creosoted wooden poles set in concrete also do well.

Tie the posts or poles together with 2- by 6-inch planks at a height of not less than 8 feet; the higher the better. An easy way to fasten the planks to iron posts is to bolt them through holes drilled at the right height. Treat the timbers with a wood preservative that is non-toxic to plants.

Snow fencing 4 feet wide makes good shade. Supports are two-by-fours laid on edge. Tack the fencing to the boards at intervals to hold it in place. If you live in an area subject to heavy snow, the fencing can be removed easily during winter. It is a good idea to enclose the exposed sides of a shade house to keep out wind and sun, but be sure to leave the front open.

In areas where there is little or no snow and wind is not severe, inexpensive shade can be provided by supporting Saran or similar material on wires. If the walks of your shade house are covered with waterproof material, such as plexiglas, customers can inspect your stock while it is raining. Concrete or asphalt walks are desirable. Muddy or dusty paths discourage many customers, especially women. Covered walkways in the shade house are appreciated by customers in wet weather. This can be accomplished by placing plastic sheets over the lath that is above the walks or aisles. Customers can then examine the plants in comfort.

Storage

You need space to store your reserve merchandise. Unless the sources of all your supplies are nearby, a backup stock is necessary, as well as a place to keep it. If outbuildings in good condition are available, it is best to use them for storing such merchandise. Otherwise, you will have to make room in the garden center building itself.

It should be pointed out, however, that quite often too much space is set aside for this purpose. It is not a good practice to stock heavily any merchandise except that which enjoys a rapid turnover. A garden center operator who makes a practice of carrying a big reserve stock may have too much invested in inventory. Stored merchandise represents inactive capital. The best practice is to carry in reserve only that amount of stock needed to take care of normal sales until a new supply can be obtained. Of course, what and how much merchandise is in this category can only be determined by experience.

Glass Houses

Give some thought to greenhouses or conservatories. While they are not essential to a profitable garden center, they can increase sales and profits. Even though you decide against one at the beginning, it would be well to provide space for it should you decide to build one later.

A good plan is to construct the greenhouse as an extension of the salesroom on the end opposite the shade house. This increases the length of your layout, making it more impressive. Having your salesroom in the center of your facilities gives customers easy access to all of your merchandise.

The garden center greenhouse is not used for growing plants but rather for their care while on display. Growing plants is a separate business, requiring separate facilities. Do not plan to grow plants in your greenhouse if you expect to sell from it. Use it for displaying houseplants, foliage plants, tropical plants and the like.

The interior arrangement of a greenhouse used for sales purposes differs from that of one used for growing plants. A good arrangement is to have an open center with plants displayed around it, thus giving the plants maximum visibility. Many large plants can be displayed so that they resemble a garden. By exercising a little ingenuity, you can make the greenhouse a very inviting area that encourages customers to spend more time in it. Most plant lovers like to browse among plants, so make it easy for them.

Greenhouses can serve satisfactorily as sales areas. This was discovered by a large wholesale plant grower. Upon deciding to go into the retail business, he removed the growing benches from one of his big greenhouses and transformed it into a garden center with surprisingly good results. Customers seemed to enjoy shopping under the glass roof.

It is customary to identify a business with a sign or signs. The first consideration, which is often overlooked, is placing the sign where customers can easily read it from a distance as they approach the garden center.

A single sign placed on a high standard in front of the garden center is often used. It should be high enough so that people can see it over intervening structures. If it is near a highway and the wording is on one plane parallel to the highway, it can not be read until customers are upon it. Rather, it should be a two-sided sign, with a minimum of words. This way, it can be read quickly.

On the other hand, the wording can be too brief. For example, a sign that reads only "Brown's" is meaningless. The business might be a hardware or clothing store. The sign should read "Brown's Garden Center" or "Brown's Nursery."

Signs placed at a distance from the highway can be read more easily and need be on only one plane. The letters should be plain and clear and the message brief. After all, the chief purpose of the sign is to identify your business.

Some garden centers use supplementary signs near entrances. These usually call attention to timely sales or are reminders that now is the time for a particular gardening practice.

You can gather valuable informa-

GARDEN CENTERS

tion by visiting other garden centers, especially those you know are successful. It would be best to call on ones in other towns, where your competition is not likely to be resented or feared. You can shop in these garden centers to see what merchandise they offer or, better still, visit with the owners or managers. Most will be glad to give you the benefit of their experience.

Selecting your stock, the plants you are going to offer for sale in your garden center, is one of your most important tasks. You need plants that are not only hardy in your area but suited to the customers' needs. Fortunately, reliable help from several sources is at hand.

Wholesale nurserymen who serve your area will welcome the opportunity to advise you. They know from experience what plants are in demand. You can depend upon them to be conscientious in their recommendations because they know that your success is in their best interests. The department of horticulture of a local state agricultural college or state university is familiar with the fruit and ornamental plants best suited to your area and will be happy to help you.

The following list includes most of the classes of nursery stock you are likely to need. It is in choosing the varieties within these categories that you will need competent help. Most of the items in this list are usually referred to as "green goods." They will be your main stock in trade.

Shade trees	Vegetable seeds
Ornamental trees	Vegetable plants
Fruit trees	Flower seeds
Nut trees	Flower plants
Small fruits	Grapevines
Evergreens	Houseplants
Broad-leaved evergreens	Foliage plants
Hedge plants	Garden roots
Roses	Berry plants
Perennials	Flower bulbs
Bedding plants	Lawn seeds
Vines	Herb seeds
Ground covers	Herb plants

There are many things gardeners need to care for their plants, such as hand tools, plant foods and pesticides. These should be carried in stock for customer convenience. A word of caution is in order, however: There is a danger of investing a disproportionate amount in accessories. The more green goods you sell, the greater the sales of accessory merchaandise. The reverse is not true. Your major source of income should be the sale of green goods.

Accessory merchandise is often referred to as "dry lines" or hard goods. The following list includes most of the items in this category. Most of these items are available from a comparatively new industry known as the garden supply industry.

Hand tools	Seeders
Shovels	Fertilizers
Spades	Plant foods
Forks	Mulches
Rakes	Fungicides
Hoes	Insecticides
Trowels	Weed killers
Pruners	Soil conditioners
Garden hoses	Potting soil
Sprayers	Sprinklers
Dusters	Watering cans

Gifts

Gifts have proven to be a profitable line of merchandise for garden centers. It is good to begin with gifts that are plant-related, such as flower bowls and vases, flower pots, planters, jardinieres and gardening books. Many other related items can be added from time to time.

There are a number of ways customers can add to their enjoyment of their outdoor living areas and patios. This can be accomplished by using some of the items on the following list. Gardeners have learned to look for these things in garden centers.

BEGINNING IN THE NURSERY BUSINESS

Garden furniture
Barbecues
Birdhouses
Bird feeders
Birdbaths
Birdseed (feed)
Fountains
Garden pottery
Planter boxes
Planter tubs
Gazing globes
Tropical fish and supplies
Garden statuary

Crafts

The sale of materials needed for handicrafts has proven a very profitable source of income for many garden centers. Among these are such crafts as flower making, flower arranging, stained glass, pottery, basket weaving, tole paining and many others. It is the practice of some garden centers to conduct classes in various crafts. Participants buy the needed materials at the center.

Christmas Business

A surprising development in the garden center industry is the great success in selling decorative Christmas merchandise. It is unlikely that anyone involved in the early days of the business had any inkling of this merchandise's potential. Many garden centers are reaping handsome profits from its sale. Indeed, some operators report that their Christmas sales are the most profitable sales of the year. This is possible because this merchandise is rarely found in variety, department or discount stores. This category includes a wide selection of Christmas tree decorations, lights of all kinds; a wide variety of candles; natural and artificial wreaths; wall, table and mantel decorations, and much, much more.

This Christmas merchandise, much of it imported, is available from specialty companies, which hold shows in large cities, usually during midsummer. Garden center buyers attend these shows to place their orders, which are shipped long before Christmas to give the centers plenty of time to price and display the merchandise. Because of the great variety of materials offered, it is difficult to decide what and how much to buy. Usually, women have better judgement than men in deciding what appeals to customers. Therefore, most of this merchandise is bought by women.

Competition in the Christmas tree business is severe, often cutthroat. Nowadays, trees are sold by supermarkets, discount stores, fraternal organizations, civic clubs, youth groups and so on. Consequently, garden centers should remove themselves from this competition by offering only the best. Artificial trees are available that are so skillfully made that they closely resemble the real thing.

Natural trees vary widely in quality. Only the best should be offered. Flocked trees sell readily. Trees that are fully decorated sell as a unit. Some garden centers deliver their trees, set them up and decorate them. Living evergreen trees, balled in earth or in tubs have a special appeal. If kept indoors only a very few days, they can be planted immediately after they have served as Christmas trees.

Artificial Flowers

Many garden centers are doing good business selling artificial flowers and plants. The popularity of this material increases as its quality improves. It is often difficult to distinguish between artificial and real plants without touching them. Artificial flowers are now used in many ways, including bouquets, set pieces, wall vases, flower boxes and table decorations. Some garden centers employ floral designers who use artificial flowers exclusively. They make arrangements to order and attractive set pieces for display in the garden shop. Only the best-quality flowers should be used. They command the highest prices and give lasting satisfaction.

There are many plants besides flowers that are faithfully reproduced, including ferns, palms, vines, shrubs, trees and even evergreens. Most of these are high-priced, but they seem to be sold readily.

Power Tools

Many customers need lawn mowers. You have to decide whether to stock them. Selling lawn mowers and other power tools can add to your profits. Some garden centers offer extended lines of power equipment. In addition to lawn mowers and edgers, you can sell garden tractors, tillers or cultivators; chain saws; log splitters; or snow throwers. Some of these have little or no relation to merchandise people expect to find in garden centers.

There are other considerations. All power equipment requires service at one time or another. Buyers expect to get this service from the store that sold the equipment. This means that you must have your own repair shop or make arrangements with someone else to do repair work for you. If you refuse to provide this service, you will alienate the customers. They will not buy power equipment or anything else you sell. Many garden center operators have decided they do not want to become repairmen and leave the power equipment business to hardware or implement dealers.

Displays

Displaying nursery stock attractively will tax your ingenuity. Evergreens, of course, do not present much of a problem. They are in full dress all year, so it is relatively easy for customers to visualize these plants in their gardens. But dormant deciduous stock is different. Customers often have to be assured that the plants are alive, for in their leafless state, they give inexperienced observers no evidence of life. These plants can be displayed with colored pictures depicting them in full dress. Descriptions should also be on the pictures. Excellent colored pictures are available for a wide range of plant varieties.

Do not display small plants in containers or pots on the ground or floor. Such a practice makes it necessary for customers to lean over or bend down to examine them. Instead, place them on tables or racks at about waist level so they can be inspected easily. Racks made with snow fencing serve very well. Large plants can be shown in beds made of 8- or 10-inch boards placed on edge. Bare-root plants, such as small shade trees, fruit trees or shrubs, should have moist packing material, such as peat, sawdust or planer shavings around their roots. Similar material should be put around the balls of B&B plants to prevent them from drying out. Do not use sand or soil, they make it too difficult to remove the plants.

There is a trend now to display evergreens and deciduous plants that are in leaf in arrangements that resemble landscape plantings. This gives customers a good idea of how these plants would look in their yards or gardens. Indeed, some garden centers display most of their plants in this fashion, and they are very impressive. Temporary demonstration gardens can be created by using container-grown or potted plants. Cover the containers with mulch.

For customer convenience, it is a good practice to display plants by classes — shrubs, evergreens and so on. Tall plants should form the background, while small ones are put in front. The primary objective is to display plants so they generate desire.

Showing related items together helps boost sales. For example, a display near the rosebushes of plant food and pesticides reminds customers that roses need these products if they are to grow and stay healthy. A pair of snips to cut flowers and a basket to hold them are amenities that appeal to rose lovers. Similar practices can be followed with many other classes of plants.

Signs

Garden centers need signs. They can provide directions or information and help sell products. Signs should make it clear where customers should park. They should also direct customers to various kinds of plants: roses, evergreens, fruit trees and so on. They can extol the merits of new plants and encourage customers to browse and to ask for help when they need it. Signs can be used in many, many ways. Avoid carelessly made signs. They offend customers. Signs should be as neat and attractive as possible. Equipment for making them is available.

Displaying Store Stock

When arranging merchandise in garden shops, group similar products. Display seeds in one place, fertilizers in another, spray material in a third and so on. Shelves can be built around the outside walls as high as people can easily reach, but floor displays are best kept low so that people can see over them.

Above all, keep your displays neat and full of merchandise. Customers are suspicious of the last can of spray material or packet of seeds. Subconsciously, they think there must be something wrong with it or it would not still be there. You sell a great deal more merchandise if your displays are as large as possible and filled with merchandise. You cannot be overly neat in your displays. A jumbled display repels customers. Good housekeeping always pays off.

If your garden center has display windows, use them to attract customers by showing some of your most desirable merchandise. Change the displays frequently, and make them as timely as possible. It should be little trouble to change displays once a month or to use merchandise that has a special appeal at a particular time. Fall bulbs are timely in October, for instance, and gift books make good reading in January.

Displays of a particular class of merchandise can be repeated, but different items within a class should be used. It is not a bad idea to change your floor displays from time to time to give the store a new look.

Frequently, customers come in to buy specific items but also buy other products they need because they happened to see them on display. Merchants call this impulse buying. You can encourage these impulses by setting up a few small displays of timely merchandise in various parts of the store. The best place for such a display is at the check-out counter. If it happens to be bulb-planting time, you can display potting soil, mulches, rodent repellents and garden labels.

Bulky Merchandise

Displaying and handling heavy, bulky merchandise always presents problems for garden centers. Large sacks of fertilizer and large bales of peat moss take up too much room in the store, and it is difficult to move them from the store to the customers' cars. Some garden merchants store such merchandise in a separate room or building directly off the parking lot.

The most convenient arrangement, of course, is to have the room or building adjoining the garden shop proper. Then, by installing large overhead garage doors on this building, you can use the storage space for fertilizers and mulches as a display and sales area whenever you want to. Arrange the bags and bales neatly around the outside wall and display smaller packages on shelves above these piles. Customers can drive their cars to the door for direct loading.

Another plan is to construct a loading dock where mulches, fertilizers and other heavy and bulky items are stored and displayed. Arrange the dock so that customers can drive alongside for loading. A covered dock may not be necessary because mulches and fertilizers are usually in waterproof bags or bales.

Plants in flats, pots or bands are best displayed on low tables or benches where it is convenient for customers to examine them. These plants should be displayed in your greenhouse if you have one. Be sure to leave plenty of aisle space in the greenhouse for convenience, especially if you provide customers with carts.

All plants should be labeled so that the customers can identify them without having to inquire. This is best accomplished with a liberal use of color pictures and descriptions next to the plants. Pictures are available in a wide assortment and of good quality. It is a good practice to label plants individually by using tags with color pictures. These tags can also show the prices.

Pricing

When pricing nursery stock and other merchandise for the first time, beginners frequently make the mistake of setting prices too low. The margin between the cost and the selling price has to cover many expenses and risks. Transportation costs, salesmen's salaries or commissions, unsold stock, shrinkage from various causes, replacements and overhead expenses are only a few.

There is no rule to follow in pricing nursery stock, but an understanding of how to figure markups will help you arrive at the right prices. The percentage of markup is based on the selling price, not on the cost. For example, if an item costs 50¢ and sells for $1, the markup is not 100 percent but 50 percent. The percentage is determined by calculating the difference between the cost and the selling price and dividing that difference by the selling price.

For most nursery stock, a 50 percent markup is not enough. A markup of $66\frac{2}{3}$ percent would be better. High-priced merchandise will not stand so great a markup as cheaper items. A shrub costing 50¢ might well retail for $1.50 or more, but an evergreen costing $15 probably cannot be sold for more than $30.

Chapter 3. Landscape Nurseries

Landscape Nurseries

Landscaping is a comparatively new practice in the US. During most of the past century, when the country was developing, the chief activities were clearing land for farming, planting orchards and just making a living. Nurseries mostly grew fruit trees at that time, and very little ornamental stock. Landscaping did not become a common practice until well into the present century. Nowadays, people do not consider their homes complete until they are landscaped. Landscaping not only beautifies homes but factories, public buildings and roadsides as well. Landscaping has become big business.

A trend today is known as naturalistic landscaping, which is an attempt to imitate nature. Natural landscapes contrast the formal plantings of the 17th and 18th centuries in England and Europe. Such gardens featured clipped hedges, fountains, statuary and geometric flower gardens. The little landscaping done in this country in the past was mostly formal.

The change began in England early in the 18th century, when the formal plantings of many large estates were destroyed. In their places appeared naturalistic plantings. So drastic were the changes that nurserymen were accused of encouraging the practice so that they could find a market for their "surplus nursery stock." At any rate, the change was permanent, and today we are blessed with pleasing and useful natural plantings.

Landscaping can be compared to home building. An architect designs a home, and a contractor builds it according to the plan. In landscaping, a landscape architect designs a planting, and a landscape nurseryman carries it out. In practice, however, very few homes and very few home landscapes are designed by professional architects. Such professionals are mostly concerned with large projects. Today, landscape nurserymen not only do the planting but most of the designing as well.

Landscape nurseries have been around for a long time but in small numbers until this century. Growing and selling fruit trees constituted most nursery activity in the 19th century. Interest in home landscaping grew tremendously with the development of garden centers. It is only logical for garden centers to serve their customers by doing their plantings. However, many garden centers were not able to provide this service. The landscape nursery evolved to fill this void.

The terms landscape architect, landscape gardener and landscaper need defining. A landscape architect is a person who has had professional training from an institution of higher learning. Many universities offer 4 year degrees in landscape architecture. Some programs require more time. The courses are designed to train students in the principles of plant designs. Students also become familiar with a wide range of plants.

The terms landscape gardener and landscaper are used loosely, and their meaning is not always clear. Usually, they refer to individuals who represent themselves as people qualified to design and plant landscapes.

A landscape nursery, for the purpose of this discussion, is one that derives the major portion of its income from designing and planting landscapes. It is a distinct business although it is often connected with other types of nursery operations and most often m with garden centers.

If you decide to enter the landscape business, your next move is to decide on a location. Like cash-and-carry nurseries and garden centers, landscape nurseries should be located near fairly large population centers. Choose a city with a high percentage of homeowners; renters are not your customers. Small cities probably have a higher percentage of homeowners than do large cities,

LANDSCAPE NURSERIES

but there are not enough homeowners to support a lively landscape business. However, a small town that is close to a number of other towns or a large city might prove successful.

Location

Locating your landscape nursery on a trafficway or busy highway is desirable but not essential, because in most cases, landscapers go to their customers to make their contacts. A large amount of business is done by telephone. Some customers may never see your place of business, and it is not necessary that they do. Landscape customers, unlike cash-and-carry buyers, are looking for service. They want you to study their problems, make recommendations and act upon them. This means you have to visit their homes or offices.

Be sure you have plenty of room for present and future needs. In addition to office facilities, you should have adequate housing for equipment, such as cars, trucks, tree movers and small tools. If you plan to grow some of your own nursery stock, you need still more land. Land in or adjacent to the corporate limits of a city is likely to be high-priced. Therefore, to make a smaller initial investment, you may want to move farther from the city.

An ideal arrangement to make when you start your landscape business would be to buy or rent a small, improved site outside the city, live there and have your office in the house. This way, you can start the business with the smallest initial investment possible.

After you have sold a number of landscape jobs, you can buy the stock necessary to plant them.

You can then gradually accumulate a modest capital, which will allow you to acquire the equipment you need to do first-class landscape work. Many landscape nurserymen have entered the business in this way.

If you rent land and plan to grow some of your own stock, your lease should be for five or more years. It would be a good idea to arrange for an option to renew the lease or buy the land when the lease ends. Moving a nursery is a big, expensive, unsatisfying job, especially if it is done on short notice.

Make it easy for prospective clients to find you. Do not assume that they know your business or location. Advertise in the classified section of the local telephone directory. Include your exact location and directions for reaching it. Put signs along the highway, and make them neat and dignified. Erect a sign at the entrance to your grounds so that customers know they have arrived, and then guide them to your office with additional signs.

As a landscape nurseryman, you should practice what you preach. Landscape your grounds to the best of your ability. Shabby, unkempt, poorly planted grounds make a bad impression on customers. On the other hand, you can demonstrate your ability as a designer by doing a good job of planting your grounds. Give special consideration to the arrangements around your office or home because customers are most likely to see and remember them.

The grounds you landscape will constitute your display. They are the show windows of your business. A well-landscaped site is one of your best advertisements. Your landscaping can be as extensive as you wish and include demonstration plantings of various types, such as formal, informal, rose and perennial gardens.

Landscape nurserymen are naturally tempted to make their demonstration plantings as elaborate as possible. While we have no objection to this plan, be sure the landscaping does not become a burden. Such plantings are expensive to install and more expensive to maintain.

BEGINNING IN THE NURSERY BUSINESS

There is a perennial argument between landscape architects and nurserymen. Landscape architects maintain that nurserymen are not qualified to design landscapes or to prepare planting plans. Nurserymen maintain that landscape architects are not realistic enough — that they specify plants ill-adapted to the location or that are unavailable. The ideal arrangement for customers might be to have well-trained professional landscape architects design the plans and skillful, experienced landscape gardeners install the plantings. But such arrangements would leave most people without any landscape service at all. Only a small percentage of homeowners can afford, or think they can afford, the expense of hiring both professional landscape architects and gardeners.

We need not concern ourselves with the merits of these arguments. You job is to give customers the best service you can. If you think a client is well able to pay for professional landscape services, perhaps you will want to advise him to hire a landscape architect. As a matter of fact, many nurseries employ landscape architects. Your part will be to install the plans after they have been prepared.

It must be acknowledged that much poor landscaping has been done by nurserymen. All too commonly, homes are landscaped with upright evergreens at each corner and spreading evergreens in between. Eventually, the corner trees become overgrown Christmas trees higher than the house despite occasional shearing. The evergreens in between become big, green marshmallows that obscure the windows.

Merely by designating their businesses as landscape nurseries, nurserymen do not escape the responsibility of being qualified as landscape designers. At least they must be able to design home plans.

Experienced nurserymen have an advantage, as they are already familiar with the plants that are needed to create a landscape. Some untrained individuals have natural artistic abilities that help them visualize fine landscape plantings entirely in their minds. They do not need to draw plans unless clients ask for them.

Always keep in mind that you must first become familiar with the trees, shrubs and plants that are the real pigments in a landscape picture. Visit nurseries as often as you can to become well-acquainted with the many plant varieties that are available. Perhaps the best and fastest way to become familiar with trees, shrubs and other plants used in landscaping is to get a job in a nursery or garden center that offers a wide assortment of plants. Working with plants every day, you will soon learn to recognize them.

Keep in mind, however, that the plants used for landscaping vary greatly from area to area. If, for example, you become familiar with the plants used in New England, that knowledge would be of little help to you in southern California, where the vegetation differs greatly from that of New England.

There is an ever increasing number of vocational and technical schools being established across the country. Many offer courses in horticulture that include some exposure to landscape design and plant identifiction. Many graduates of these schools have become successful landscape nurserymen.

No matter how proficient you may become in design, that skill will be useless unless you know what plants to use in your designs. A landscape architect unfamiliar with plants is like a painter who is color-blind. The landscape picture, unlike the oil painting, is constantly changing. If it is to be pleasing during all seasons, the appearance of the plants at various times of the year must be considered.

Not only must landscape architects know the colors and textures of their plants (just as painters must know the colors and textures of their paints), they must also know much more. People who would create pleasing landscape pictures should be familiar with the hardiness of the plants they specify, their ability to grow in shade or sun, the ultimate heights to which they grow, the textures of their foliages, their appearances in different seasons and any other qualities they possess.

There are numerous good books on landscape design. A conscientious study of one or more would be rewarding. At times, certain universities offer correspondence courses on the subject. Finally, a study of good landscape plantings in your area would also be helpful.

Homeowners are the Best Customer

You can have a wide variety of customers in the landscape business. Homeowners usually constitute the most important group. Owners of new homes are the best prospects because the idea that a home is not complete until it is planted has been well-publicized.

The landscape nursery industry is, in reality, closely attuned to the home building industry. Millions of new homes have to be built to supply the needs of a rapidly growing population. A very high percentage of these homes will be landscaped, and this percentage is constantly increasing. More and more homeowners are becoming aware of the desirability of having their homes landscaped. Beautiful surroundings add to a homeowner's feeling of well-being. Landscaping adds a great deal more than its cost to the resale value of a home. Landscaping can increase a home's comfort by providing cooling shade in summer and protection from cold winds in winter.

Many homes were landscaped so long ago that the plantings are in poor condition or utterly out of date. Landscapes become old-fashioned and wear out just as hats and cars do. Such plantings should be torn out and replaced with new material. Therefore, old homes constitute a large potential market in addition to new ones.

An engaging idea in landscape design is the outdoor living room. So much has been written about this concept in garden magazines and the daily press that the public is well-informed. Fundamentally, the outdoor living room is an area, usually at the rear of the house, which is set aside for relaxation. Border plantings are heavy enough to ensure privacy. This area is used for reading, lounging and so on. It lends itself to a great variety of treatments, which depend upon the tastes and wishes of the owners. Most outdoor living areas require considerable quantities of nursery stock.

Another popular feature in home landscaping is the patio. This feature usually adjoins the house for easy access. It is a paved area, often with overhead shade. A table and chairs allow owners to relax, visit, take coffee breaks, lunch and even dine. Landscaping patios in pleasing ways challenges the ingenuity of nurserymen. It should be well-shaded with trees, and its borders should be decorated with low-growing plants and flowers. Containers and potted plants are ideal because the plantings can be redesigned easily.

Sometimes a landscape includes one or several features: walls, steps, walks, fish pools, lily ponds, fountains and even swimming pools. Previously, such elements were usually constructed by separate contractors. Now landscape nurserymen do this work as part of their overall contracts. This means you have to develop these skills or subcontract the work.

Lawns are now part of many contracts to landscape homes. Therefore, lawn-making is a skill that landscape nurserymen need at times. Consequently, you should be informed as thoroughly as possible. Valuable help is available from the agricultural extension services of most state universities, where you can learn about soil problems, fertilizers and grasses, as well as the proper care of a new lawn. Clients may want you to install a sprinkling system. Some landscape nurserymen can, but some cities require licensed plumbers to do this work.

You will discover that many homeowners, especially those with new homes, want to do their own landscaping. A survey conducted jointly by National Home Center News and the National Association of Home Builders revealed that at least 50 percent of the owners of new homes thought of landscaping as a do-it-yourself project. Landscape nurserymen can profit by helping such homeowners plan their landscaping and by furnishing the plant materials. Older homes that have never been landscaped or that need renovating offer similar opportunities to landscape nurserymen.

It is a common practice to landscape apartment buildings. Renters can enjoy the greenery without having any responsibility for its care. Landscaping apartment complexes consisting of several buildings are often major projects, which involve planting shade and flowering trees and flower gardens and constructing pools, running water systems and fountains.

Churches, schools and hospitals are extensive markets for landscape nurserymen. Usually, these institutions have plans drawn by professional landscape architects and then advertise for bids. All too often, building architects attempt to prepare the plans so that they can earn the additional fees. But most building architects are no better qualified to prepare landscape plans than landscape architects are to design buildings. Therefore, specifications prepared by building architects are often difficult, if not impossible, to meet. Plantings based on such specifications are not satisfactory and may reflect adversely on the skill of the nurserymen who install them.

Before bidding on any large project that involves a considerable sum of money, you should inspect the grounds. Evaluate the soil condition, presence of rocks, necessary grading, the availability and cost of labor, whether you can run trucks into the grounds (you might have to use a wheelbarrow) and the utilities you will need to use. A successful bidder may lose money on a job by overlooking some items that cause unforeseen expenses. Any questionable matters not covered by the specifications in the plan should be cleared up before you bid on the project.

Some landscape projects may require certain plants that are not grown by nurserymen in your area and that you are unable to find. This should be explained to the client. If possible, arrange for a substitute. Such matters may be referred to the landscape architects who specified the plants. A typical reaction is, "That is a good plant, and nurserymen should be growing it." Of course, it is not practical for nurserymen to grow all the "good" plants. Sometimes substitutions are necessary, but clients should agree to them.

Above all, remember that it is better not to bid on a project at all than to bid dangerously low in fear of being underbid by a competitor. You cannot stay in business long if you merely trade dollars with clients or operate at a loss. Let other landscapers have a few jobs below cost. They will not offer serious competition for very long.

It is true that a few landscape nurserymen enter low bids, planning to chisel on the specifications. Not only is such a practice grossly dishonest, it is not even intelligent. Inevitably, it harms the bidder. In the long run, the best advertisement a landscape nurseryman can have is a well-done job. Any landscape nurseryman who has been in the business long will tell you that the best business comes from people who have seen the work the company has done. Enthusiastic customers are always ready to recommend you. On the other hand, the unfavorable advertising of a skimpy job more than offsets any profit you might have made with questionable practices.

Cemeteries frequently need the services of landscape nurserymen. New cemetery areas need trees along the drives and shrubs or hedges around the outer boundaries. The latest idea in cemeteries is the memorial park, which simulates a beautiful, well-landscaped park.

Monuments are either entirely prohibited in a memorial park or permitted only in restricted areas. Lots are not outlined by curbs, grilles, fences or hedges or in any other way. Markers set flush with the ground indicate the location of the graves. The overall effect is more restful and comforting than the forest of monuments that confronts people in old-fashioned cemeteries. Memorial parks use their grounds more economically and lend themselves to more pleasing landscape treatments.

The modern concept of useful, living memorial parks instead of cemeteries with monuments or statues is meeting with public approval. Conscientious landscape nurserymen who are commissioned to design or plant such parks do their best to create ones that serve the needs of the public. Only the longest-living and best adapted trees and shrubs should be used in such areas.

Cemetery designing is a highly developed art, involving a thorough knowledge of landscape design, as well as considerable engineering skill. It is better to leave this job to professional designers unless you are willing to spend a lot of time preparing for it.

Industrial Landscaping

Industry leaders are learning that workers are more efficient in attractive, restful surroundings. When big industries erect factories, assembly plants, warehouses and research centers, they routinely have the sites landscaped. Many jobs are extremely well-done, making the grounds look like parks. The owners of some of the modern industrial sites that are leased, rather than sold, landscape the new buildings as part of their services to tenants. They would not spend money in this way unless they considered it a profitable investment.

To provide pleasant surroundings for their workers, some industrialists have cleaned up and landscaped the grounds around factories that have been operating for many years. So much importance is currently attached to landscaping that people sometimes see extremely valuable land adjoining new buildings in downtown areas set aside for gardens.

Landscape nurserymen will find that park, airport, subdivision and housing projects are lucrative markets. It pays to keep yourself well-informed on such developments in your area so that you can take advantage of the opportunity to bid on them. Become well-acquainted with your city officials, park commissioners, contractors, home builders and real estate developers so that they will think of you when they need the services of a landscape nurseryman.

Remain alert to trends in home architecture. Changes in styles may require a different type of landscape treatment and call for trees and shrubs other than those that were previously in demand. For instance, two-story cape cod homes cannot be given the same treatment as modern ranch-style houses — the majority of homes built since World War II. Because they have lower lines than cape cods, ranch houses need lower-growing plants about them, such as semidwarf and even dwarf species.

Plants enjoy vogues, just as dresses do. Styles in plants change more slowly, of course, than do fashions in dresses, but sometimes the changes come before nurserymen are fully aware of them.

Taxus species are replacing several other kinds of evergreens in popularity. The use of some common shrubs in foundation and border planting is declining. On the other hand, broad-leaved evergreens are being used more liberally. Do not try to run counter to these trends; they reflect customer preference.

You will discover that customers want something new in plants. They will visit you to ask, "What is new?" They really are interested in something different, which, when planted in their gardens, become conversation pieces or novelties to show their friends. This is a healthy interest, one you should encourage and try to satisfy by keeping up-to-date on desirable new plants and making them available.

If there are wholesale nurseries near you, visit them and ask about new introductions. Search wholesale nursery catalogs for new plants you believe would interest your customers. Desirable new plants are often described in nursery trade journals, which you should be reading. If there is an arboretum near you, be sure to visit it for help in finding new and desirable plants.

Magazines and newspapers wield a strong influence in shaping public demand. A skillfully written and cleverly illustrated article might create a demand that nurserymen may have difficulty satisfying.

The garden magazines in the US have many millions of readers who become better informed every year. You should subscribe to and read these magazines to keep up with the customers' thinking. Daily papers in large cities cater to their readers by maintaining garden departments. Nurserymen ought to be grateful for all this publicity, because it is making the US a nation of gardeners.

Selling landscape services requires different tactics than does selling nursery stock in a cash-and-carry salesyard, where customers are primarily interested in individual plants. Landscape clients think in terms of results. When working with a prospective landscape customer, try to paint a word picture. Talk in terms of beautiful lawns, colorful gardens and restful outdoor living rooms. Prospects are not interested in knowing you would plant a group of shrubs here, a tree there and a screen somewhere else. They are more interested in the scenes you will create with your plantings.

Try not to mention cost until you have done your best to create such a strong desire for the landscape planting that expense becomes a secondary matter. During such discussions, you can probably get a fairly accurate idea of how much clients are willing to spend. If they think they cannot afford to carry out entire plantings at one time, suggest doing them over two or three years. If you do, you should always adhere to the original plans so that the plantings have unity when they are done.

Drawing Plans

It costs money to draw plans. An elaborate plan is usually not necessary for the average home grounds consisting of only two or three city lots. You can sit down with a client, learn any preferences and then draw a rough sketch of how you propose to develop the property. Often this is the only plan you need to draw. You have to work out the details of what to plant, where and how many so that you can make an intelligent estimate of the cost, but these details are for your own information.

You will encounter prospects who are shoppers; they are a real nuisance in the landscape business. They demand detailed plans, which they promise to take home and study. They then go to your competitors and get plans from them. After they have acquired several plans, they may decide to buy the stock from other nurserymen and plant it themselves, according to whichever plan they like best. They may even turn your plan and quotation over to a competitor who is willing to underbid you to get the job and use your plan.

To avoid such situations, tell prospects that plans remain your property and must be returned within a reasonable length of time if they decide not to buy. You can further protect yourself by making the planting list separate from the design plan. Retain this list yourself until the job is yours. The ideal procedure is to charge for plans, a practice followed by many nurseries. As an inducement to the customer to give you his business, you can offer to apply the cost of the plan to the cost of the landscape job.

Plant Carefully

Use high-quality, strong plants in your landscape plantings. The difference between the costs of poor stock and good stock makes comparatively little difference in the cost of the job. Good stock makes a better-looking planting and is more likely to grow. You cannot satisfy customers and build enduring goodwill by cutting corners.

Do your planting carefully. Have a qualified person supervise the work to ensure it is done properly. It is not enough to stake out jobs and then leave them in the hands of day laborers. Trees, shrubs and especially evergreens must be planted at exactly the right depths. Some pruning is always necessary to remove broken roots and branches or to balance the top with the roots.

Be neat. Leave a clean-cut line between the lawn and the area you planted. Level the soil around new plantings, remove surplus soil, sweep off walks and drives, and clean up all debris. Show customers that you take pride in your work.

Explain to clients that nursery stock is perishable and that, like any other living thing, it needs care and attention. They know that baby chicks and puppies must have good care to survive, but they are likely to think that trees and shrubs take care of themselves. Show them how to water, cultivate, prune and spray. Give them all the instructions they can absorb. Your effort will pay dividends. The more personal attention customers give their plants, the more interest they are likely to take in them, and the better the plants' chances for survival will be.

Guarantees

A problem you may encounter on your first job is one that still causes heated discussions among nurserymen — guaranteeing. Most customers want to know if you guarantee your stock to grow. You have to formulate some sort of policy and follow it consistently.

Associations of landscape nurserymen in some cities and states have adopted standard forms of guarantees. If such a guarantee is used in your city or state, you should adopt it, too. These guarantees are the results of long experience and are probably the best that can be worked out for the regions in which they apply.

If there is no standard guarantee in your area, you will have to work out one for yourself. A plan that some nurserymen have followed successfully is to quote two prices on landscape jobs — one with a guarantee and one without. The former might be 20 to 25 percent higher than the latter. The extra cost represents a premium on insurance that protects the purchaser against loss. If any stock fails to survive the first growing season after planting, it is replaced free.

Regardless of the plan you adopt, you should bear in mind the fact that you can never expect 100 percent survival in your plantings. Consequently, if you offer any guarantee at all, you must protect yourself by charging enough to cover this hazard. We suggest that you discuss this matter with successful landscape nurserymen in your vicinity and profit by their advice.

It is a good plan to continue to show interest in landscape jobs after you have completed them. Inspect the sites occasionally yourself or send an employee. Visit with clients about their landscapes. Tell them what they need to know to properly care for their properties. This way, you can keep your planting losses to a minimum. Your clients will be grateful for your interest and be more likely to recommend you to other people.

If you want to keep workers busy during summer when there is little landscape planting, give serious thought to offering a yard service. There is a real need for this service, and it can be very profitable. It would consist of pruning trees, shrubs and evergreens; spraying to control diseases and insects; fertilizing; and lawn care. In short, a lawn service does everything necessary for the proper care of a home landscape planting. Employees would have to be trained to do the work properly, and you would need special equipment. Rendering satisfactory service could lead to contracts to renovate tired old plantings or even to do entirely new ones.

Should You Grow or Buy Stock

Perhaps you are wondering whether you should grow your own nursery stock. In many cases, a landscape business requires a wide variety of stock, including shade trees, evergreens, shrubs, hedge plants, vines, roses and perennials. Much skill, time, equipment and supervision is required not only to propagate nursery stock but also to plant, cultivate, trim, spray, dig and store it properly. Unless you are prepared to set up an organization to do all this, it would be better to buy your nursery stock. In this way, your risk would be minimal because you would not need to buy a considerable quantity of stock until you had orders for it.

Under certain circumstances, you may find it advantageous to have some nursery stock growing on your own grounds, especially large shade trees and evergreens, which are expensive to ship and difficult to store. Landscape clients often want to see the trees that are specified for their jobs and may even want to select them themselves. In such a case, it is an advantage to have trees growing on your own grounds.

You do not need a large stock to impress clients because the average layman does not have a clear idea of what constitutes a nursery. Comparatively few trees look like many to a layman, and a large assortment may only confuse clients. Have you ever gone into a large clothing store to buy a suit only to find such a large array that you became confused and had difficulty making up your mind? For this reason, even if you are growing a wide variety of nursery stock, it is advisable to create a display area in which only a limited selection is growing.

Businessmen who have similar interests often form organizations so that they can benefit from exchanging ideas, fostering legislation, promoting business and so on. Landscape nurserymen are no exception. They banded together a number of years ago to form a national organization now known as the National Landscape Association.

It is a strong group with members in all parts of the country. It has an aggressive program under the management umbrella of the American Association of Nurserymen. When you have established your business we suggest you apply for membership; the benefits will be many.

Chapter 4. Agency Nurseries

Agency Nurseries

Retail nurseries that sell their products through salesmen are known as agency nurseries. The salesmen are called agents. For more than 100 years, the agency nursery dominated the retail nursery business. More nursery stock was sold to consumers by agency nurseries than by all other methods combined. It should be made clear that the agents who sold the nursery stock were not employees of the nurseries. Instead, they were paid commissions on their sales. In other words, the agents were independent operators. However, the nursery industry was dependent upon them for marketing its products.

Because it was not practical for the agents to carry samples of their wares, some carried specimens of fruits preserved in alcohol in glass jars and had hand-painted pictures of fruits and flowers. The preserved fruits were rarely typical of what customers could expect to grow on their own trees, and the pictures were gaudy exaggerations. It was not until late in the last century that good representative pictures were available. Agents carried many of these pictures bound together in such a fashion that the whole array could be spread out at once.

During the last century and the early days of this century, when most of the people lived on farms, agents went from farm to farm via horse and buggy or on horseback. They often stayed overnight with the farmer and gave the farmer's wife a rose bush or shrub as payment. Farms needed orchards if the owners wanted fresh fruit. There were few commercial orchards, and fresh fruit was rarely found in the stores. The result was that most farms had orchards.

Unfortunately, some agents were not strictly honest. To make sales, they would misrepresent the plants they offered or make promises of which the nurseries they represented were unaware. While the practice was not condoned by nurserymen, it reflected on the integrity of the nurseries involved. This unfortunate situation existed for a long time in the earlier days of the nursery industry.

Nevertheless, the country owes a debt of gratitude to the tree agents and to the nurseries they represented for making possible the farm orchards, shelterbelts, windbreaks and woodlots, as well as the occasional spots of beauty filled with roses and flowers.

When most of the country became urban instead of rural, the nursery agents followed the people into town. They went from house to house, selling fruit tres for the back yard. Even then, fruit trees were still needed. By that time, beautiful color photographs of the flowers and fruits were available to the agents. Dishonest agents became a rarity, and the nursery agency business prospered.

One of the agents' practices, which was done in cooperation with the nurseries they represented, was to photograph the prospect's home and send the pictures to the nursery, along with rough dimensions of the grounds. The nursery prepared a simple plan that the agent could present and sell to the homeowner as a do-it-yourself project. Many homes were beautified in this manner when professional landscaping was almost unknown. The agency nursery during the first quarter of this century was a big, thriving enterprise.

It is likely that many people reading this never heard of agency nurseries. If they were of great importance for such a long time, why is it, they may ask, that we do not hear about them now? That is a good question, and we will try to answer it.

The prosperity of the retail nursery industry during the first quarter of the present century was due largely to the activities of the nursery salesmen or agents. There were thousands of thcm selling for nurseries in all parts of the country. Many of the oldest and largest nurseries in operation today began as agency nurseries. Even then, fruit trees were more important than ornamental plants.

Then came the Great Depression, which began in the late 1920s and climaxed in the mid-1930s. Beginning about that time and continuing until the close of World War II, changes took place that amounted to a revolution in nursery stock marketing.

Due to the bad state of the economy, nursery agents found it increasingly difficult to make sales. When they could no longer support themselves by selling nursery stock, they simply stopped trying and looked for other work. They had no financial investment in the nurseries, and therefore nothing to lose. The exodus of salesmen from the nursery business was so great that some of the largest agency nurseries in the US went out of business. Many other nurseries that depended upon agents for at least part of their sales were forced to seek other methods of marketing their products. The end of the practice of selling nursery stock by agents was in sight.

Because agents were no longer calling on them, people in the country and in towns had to depend on local nurseries (if there were any) for trees, shrubs and other plants. No longer experiencing competition from agents, these nurseries enjoyed improved sales, however small that increase might have been. The more alert nurserymen soon realized that home gardeners needed certain accessories to properly care for their plants.

Up to then, people had to go to the hardware store for shovels, hoes and rakes. For pesticies, the drug store was their source. They might buy fertilizers and mulches from the feed store. Why shouldn't the nursery provide all of these? The progressive nurseries adopted this practice; the concept of the modern garden center was born. The concept was to make available everything customers needed for gardening.

Mail-order nurseries also benefitted from the quickly disappearing agency competitiion. Increasing notably in number, mail-order nurseries served wide areas of the country that had no nurseries. By the end of World War II, local nurseries and mail-order companies were increasingly healthy. The practice of selling nursery stock by agents was all but gone.

Chapter 5. Mail-Order Nurseries

Mail-Order Nurseries

Mail-order nurserymen have been around for a long time. They were pioneers in the mail-order business. The first nursery catalog of record was issued in 1771 by Prince Nursery on Long Island in New York. It offered only fruit trees — at 33¢ each! Prince Nursery, North America's first nursery, was established in 1750 and published many catalogs throughout its 100 years.

Because it was difficult to visit nurseries in those early days of primitive transportation, orders were placed by mail. Nursery stock could be delivered by ship to settlements on the coast and on rivers that flowed into the sea. Early in the 18th century, canals began serving wide areas. It was not long before railroads were reaching more people, too.

Nurseries were springing up at a rapid pace all over the East. Most offered fruit trees and fruit plants only. By the middle of the century, hundreds of thousands of fruit trees were being produced yearly. Some catalogs offered garden and field seeds as well. Nurseries have been issuing catalogs ever since.

One of the most fascinating ways to sell nursery stock is by mail. If you think you have any talent for advertising, merchandising, sales-letter writing or catalog building, the mail-order business will afford you a good opportunity to demonstrate it.

Some people are temperamentally unable to deal with the public face-to-face, as successful over-the-counter retailers must, but they can write letters that will please customers. If you are such a person, we suggest the mail-order business rather than any other type of nursery business because mail-order nurserymen rarely see the customers.

We should say at the outset that you have to build your mail-order business rather slowly, unless you are prepared to make a considerable initial investment. It takes a lot of money to print catalogs that will pull orders. About the only way to build an effective mailing list is to conduct an advertising campaign, and such campaigns are costly.

From the very beginning of the US nursery industry, most nursery stock was sold by salesmen, usually called agents, who went door-to-door. During the first quarter of the 20th century, some nurseries employed thousands of these agents. However, by the middle of the Great Depression in the 1930s, this business was practically wiped out. Agents could not make sales, and they turned to other activities. A number of the largest nurseries went out of business.

Before 1925, mail-order nurseries were counted in the dozens. By 1950, they numbered in the hundreds. This phenomenal growth can be attributed partly to the demise of the agency nursery. Furthermore, the garden center business was still in its infancy; it offered little competition.

Then, the mail-order business saw a gradual decline. Many large companies, including two of the world's largest mercantile companies, discontinued their mail-order nursery businesses entirely. It is generally believed that this decline was largely due to the growth of local nurseries and garden centers. Today, there are probably fewer than 100 active mail-order nurseries. However, some are highly successful, issuing hundreds of thousands of catalogs and generating large volumes of business.

An exciting new trend is developing in marketing. As reported by Time magazine, "Catalogs have become a major factor in the US economy;" they are influencing the buying habits of Americans. This influence is demonstrated by the fact that catalog sales are increasing more rapidly than are in-store sales. Time estimated that more than 5 billion catalogs were mailed in 1982, offering a vast assortment of merchandise.

It appears that Americans are learning to enjoy shopping by mail and avoiding the time and inconvenience of visiting the stores competing for attention. Shopping by catalog can be done leisurely and in comfort. Beautiful illustrations and enticing descriptions can help customers decide on their purchases. If the trend to shop by catalog has a favorable influence on the nursery catalog business remains to be seen, but it is pleasant to assume that it will.

There are a number of reasons why mail-order nurseries are finding it difficult to compete with local nurseries and garden centers. Railway express service entirely disappeared a few years ago. Parcel post rates have steadily risen, while the service has deteriorated. There is some relief, as truck freight service is available. United Parcel Service and Merchants Delivery are providing better delivery services.

Another problem faced by mail-order nurseries is the increased cost of printing catalogs. The extensive use of expensive color is essential for best results. Unless very large runs are possible, the unit cost soon becomes prohibitive.

Still another difficulty encountered in developing a mail-order business is the high cost of advertising required to build mailing lists. The advertising rates of top-quality magazines, which attract the best customers, are very high. You may have noted that, with few exceptions, mail-order nursery advertisements in these magazines are quite small and in black and white.

Some mail-order nurseries have discontinued publishing expensive catalogs and depend on large advertisements in magazines and newspapers. Such ads often offer numerous popular items at rather low prices.

The most rapid development of the mail-order nursery business was concurrent with the early growth of radio broadcasting. Direct selling by radio reached its peak in the Roaring 20s. Many people enjoyed the novelty of shopping on the air. But nurseries soon found that to get the greatest benefit from their radio advertising, they had to follow up by sending catalogs to the customers. Today, direct selling of nursery stock by radio is practically nonexistent.

The season for catalog sales is comparatively short, comprising just the spring months. However, some catalog nurseries are now issuing catalogs in midspring and fall.

If you are still interested in building a mail-order business after reading about these rather disturbing developments, the following discussion should prove helpful.

Catalog Use is Greater

There are still many towns all over the country — even some that are fairly large — that have no nurseries. The people in these towns either have to drive considerable distances to buy their trees and shrubs or buy by mail. The latter method is chosen by many because it is easier.

Mail-order nurseries have an advantage not enjoyed by other nursery outlets. They are able to offer customers much wider assortments of plants because they do not have to display their stock. The assortment a garden center or salesyard can offer is limited by the amount of display space available.

Nursery catalogs are mailed at the end of the year or very early in the next. This gives the recipients many long winter evenings to pore over the catalog leisurely. The illustrations and the descriptions help customers decide what they want to buy.

Your mailing list is your most valuable asset. You should devote your utmost skill and most careful attention to building it. There are several ways to secure names for your list. You may decide to use any or all of them.

First, heed this word of caution. It may occur to you that a good way to get a mailing list is to buy one. There are companies in the business of building mailing lists for many businesses, including the nursery business. It might be possible for you to buy a list of people who purchased nursery stock by mail, but it would be a disappointment. These folks are not your customers. The fact that they have bought from one catalog is no assurance that they will buy from you. The risk is too great, and it is better not to go that route.

Two Goals

There are two theories of advertising nursery stock for the retail trade. One holds that the advertisements should offer specific items for sale, stating the price and soliciting orders. In this way, advertisers obtain names for their mailing lists, and the profits from the sales help defray the costs of the advertisements.

The other theory upholds the institutional type of advertising. Specific items may or may not be offered, but the chief purpose of the ad is to arouse enough interest in the advertiser's product that readers are spurred to action — requesting a catalog. The chief purpose of any advertising you do will be to build your mailing list with the names of people you know are interested in nursery stock. Your problem will be to decide what kind of advertising to do — direct selling, institutional or both — and what media to use — newspapers or magazines.

The kind of nursery stock you plan to sell and the territory in which you want to sell it are prime considerations in deciding how to spend your advertising budget. Let us suppose you have decided you want to sell mostly fruit trees and fruit plants. Obviously, your best markets are not in large cities or urban areas but in small towns and farming sections. Accordingly, you would not advertise in big city newspapers but in the farm press and small town newspapers.

Selecting Media

Now let us assume that you plan to confine your territory to several states, the ones you can serve the best. Ads in magazines with national circulations would be wasteful, because inquiries would come from all over the country. Make up a list of the publications that circulate in the territory you want to develop; send for sample copies, advertising rates and circulation breakdowns. With this information, you can decide which publications will give you the best coverage.

For nationwide coverage, the garden and home magazines give best results. However, the advertising rates in most are high, so you have to use good judgment in deciding what and when to advertise and in preparing copy. Bear in mind that in magazines with large circulations, space must be reserved a long time in advance, and copy must be mailed many weeks ahead of their publication dates.

Some national magazines publish regional editions, such as Eastern, Southern, Central and Western. Space can be purchased in the editions that circulate in the location you want to develop. Therefore, it is not necessary to buy space that reaches the entire nation.

One successful mail-order nurseryman obtains most of his names from advertising in daily papers and especially in the Sunday editions of papers that maintain garden departments. He does not attempt direct selling but offers interesting novelties in several small advertisements rather than in one large ad. His theory is that he attracts more buyers by offering many items instead of featuring only one or two.

Turn to the garden section of any daily newspaper. Chances are you will find numerous advertisements offering many items of nursery stock at low prices. If you are planning to advertise on some of these same pages, you may be disturbed by what looks like severe competition, but the merchandise offered is often not worth any more than the prices that the ads quote. Shade trees that sell three for $1 are only seedlings a few inches high. Rosebushes offered for $6 a dozen are too small to meet the requirements of any standard grade and are usually not worth planting.

Bargain Competition

The buyers who fall for these bargains are almost invariably disappointed and will not knowingly buy from the same nurseries again. Consequently, the people who advertise inferior and undersized stock have to depend on new customers every year. They receive no continuing benefits from their advertising and are not building substantial businesses.

Fortunately, most customers are intelligent enough to realize that merchandise is usually worth no more than the price quoted for it in an ad. This must be true because many responsible and successful mail-order nurserymen continue to use the newspapers to advertise their products. Newspaper publishers are aware of the situation and would like to do something about it. However, as long as the ads submitted by marginal operators conform to the fair-trade practice rules for the industry, there is little the publishers can do.

Naturally, it is disconcerting to find your advertisement offering No. 1 rosebushes for $7 next to another one offering roses for $2.

Some mail-order nurseries have found radio advertising is highly effective in building their mailing lists. In fact, a few companies have been developed entirely in this way. The territory that the average radio station covers effectively is not large. Local stations cover a radius of 50 to 100 miles; only the most powerful stations can claim a radius of several hundred miles.

Advertising time on the radio is in demand so much that you may not be able to get your advertisement on the air at a time when it would be most effective. If your customers are farmers, an announcement at 10 a.m. may not be heard by many. If you are catering to people in the city, a plug at 6 a.m. will find most of your customers asleep. Because of the inflexibility of radio advertising, you may find it difficult to cover your territory efficiently by it alone.

To be most effective, any kind of advertising must be done regularly. Sporadic advertising rarely pays. It takes time to break into the consciousness of your prospects, and the best way to do this is by repetition — not necessarily of the same advertisement but of the same idea and name.

Ad Agencies

You should consider the advantages of using an advertising agency. Such an organization writes advertisements, prepares schedules, reserves space and supplies publications with copy in time for the scheduled dates. In other words, ad agencies look after all of the details. The best thing about it is that the services of an accredited advertising agency cost you exactly nothing. Publications pay agencies commissions for advertising business. Your only expenses will be the costs of the artwork, engraving and electrotypes, expenses you would have even if you handled all the details yourself.

If your advertising budget is small, you may think an agency would not be interested in handling your business. That might be true of some large agencies, but many small companies are capable of doing good work and are looking for new accounts. They know that almost all accounts start with small budgets. They also know that if they do a good job for you, your account will grow.

Do not be in a hurry to select an agency. After you have interviewed several, you will have a good idea of which one shows the most genuine interest in your business.

Writing advertising copy is a highly developed art. Advertising agencies employ skilled copywriters. This is another reason why it is an advantage to use the services of an advertising agency. Guard against exaggerated and false statements. Not only are they dishonest but also unnecessary. Reasonable, straightforward statements breed confidence and are just as persuasive as those that impose upon a reader's credulity. The buying public is intelligent; do not insult it.

Keep detailed records of your advertising results. This will help you distribute your advertising funds the following year. During your first year, you have to rely solely upon your own judgment or that of your representative at the agency, but you can eliminate a large part of the guesswork in subsequent years because you will know from experience what results to expect from each publication.

You should know how many customer inquiries each publication generates with each advertisement and from what states or areas those inquiries come. You can then determine each publiction's cost per inquiry at the end of the season by dividing the cost of the space in each by the number of responses it generated.

Some results may surprise you. For example, a publication with a high advertising rate might produce so many inquiries that the cost per inquiry is lower than that of a publication with a low advertising rate. This is true because rates are based, to a large extent, on circulation.

However, the cost per inquiry tells only part of the story. Your records should also show which inquiries turned into orders. Sometimes a publication produces a large number of inquiries of which only a few result in orders. On the other hand, some publications generate comparatively few inquiries but turn a high percentage of them into orders. The publication that has the greatest value to you is the one that produces the greatest volume of business per dollar invested in advertising. Several years of careful record keeping will be required before you have enough information to make a complete appraisal of each publication.

To obtain the information you need for your records, follow the practice known as "keying." One way is to assign each publication a letter and each advertisement a number. For instance, you might be advertising dwarf apple trees in Farmer's Friend. "A" could stand for Farmer's Friend and "6" for the dwarf apple tree advertisement. Thus when inquiries come addressd to you referring to A-6, you will know immediately what advertisement and publication your prospect read. There are many other ways to key ads. Your ingenuity will suggest several to you.

Mailing Lists

Mailing lists are best kept on cards. If only one name is placed on a card, the system can be completely flexible so that additions and deletions are easy. There are several card systems. One of the best consists of a rigid stencil instead of an ordinary card. The essential information about the customer's account is recorded on the margin of the stencil, which is made for that express purpose. The customer's name and address is cut into the stencil with a typewriter. The stencils can then be run through a machine, which addresses catalogs and other literature quickly and accurately.

For the customers in your mailing list, record on the cards the dates and sources of their original inquiries and dates and amounts of the orders they made. This information helps determine which advertising media produced the most business. Remember, the medium that generates the most inquiries is not always the one that proves the most profitable.

Large mailing lists are now computerized. Computers can be programmed not only to store all essential information but to address the catalogs as well.

Eliminate Non-Buyers

Many people who ask for catalogs never become customers. After they have received two or three catalogs without ordering, their names should be removed from your list. Some companies with large mailing lists do not mail more than one catalog unless the inquirer sends an order. You can reduce your selling costs by keeping your mailing list active and up-to-date. Established companies believe they have to sell a certain amount of merchandise per catalog to make their businesses profitable. Mailing many catalogs that bring no orders pulls that average down rapidly.

Your catalog is your salesman; as such, it is your most important publication. The most skillfully built catalog is ineffective if it is sent to the people on a poor mailing list; conversely, a carelessly written, poorly printed catalog will not produce the business you have a right to expect from a good mailing list. It is quite obvious, therefore, that for the mailing list and catalog to be effective, they both must be the product of your best efforts.

Good mail-order catalogs were printed in this country more than a century ago, but they were more like references than catalogs. They merely listed varieties of plants with their descriptions. They did not make much effort to sell the products. All that is different today. With the modern developments in the art of color printing, nurserymen are now able to illustrate their products in all their glory.

When you start to build a mail-order catalog, the first thing you should do is select the assortment you want to offer. This is a very important job. The more closely the products you offer conform to what the public wants, the easier your selling job will be. For example, suppose you are growing a certain little known variety of shrub in large quantities or are able to buy it cheaply. You decide you can make a lot of money from this shrub because of its low cost. The chances are that it will sell poorly, even at a low price. A good illustration and a snappy description will help, but the space in the catalog will probably not pay for itself.

On the other hand, given that same space, a shrub that is well-known will outsell the unknown shrub several times over. Of course, you cannot fill your catalog with varieties of equal popularity, but try to pick as many winners as possible. One way to do this is to analyze the catalogs of a number of successful mail-order companies operating in the same territory that you plan to cover. If a certain variety is listed in all or most of these catalogs, you can be fairly sure it is a popular item. Your wholesale sources can also be helpful in helping you choose the best varieties. You must make sure the varieties you select are available.

Novelties can be profitable. The most successful mail-order nurseries are constantly on the lookout for new items of proven merit. Many gardeners want new plants and are willing to pay high prices for them. But do not make the mistake of offering new items that have not been thoroughly tested in the area you serve. You will do your customers a disservice if you sell them plants that are not adapted to their conditions. And customer dissatisfaction will hurt your business.

Make your descriptions brief and concise. No one likes to read long, detailed dissertations. Put yourself in the customers' place. Try to figure out what they most want to know about your product and then tell them in your most interesting manner. Stick to the truth; do not exaggerate. Just as in advertising, a straight-forward statement is most effective.

Use numerous illustrations. A good picture is your best sales help. You have noticed how the large mail-order houses illustrate as many of their articles as they possibly can. Illustrations should be clearly captioned so that there will be no doubt as to their identities in the mind of the reader.

Consider using four-color illustrations. Probably no other product lends itself more readily to color than nursery stock. Many mail-order nursery catalogs are things of beauty with gorgeous illustrations in full color. Increasingly, mail-order nurseries are using color in their catalogs. Many are using full color.

Catalog Costs

Among the largest single costs of producing a catalog are those of composition and makeup. Composition is the task of setting of your copy into type. Any mistakes in the original copy that you supply the printer has to be corrected later. Making corrections after the type has been set is expensive. Therefore, you should prepare your copy carefully to eliminate as many mistakes as possible.

Makeup is the task of assembling the type and illustrations for printing. The type has to be arranged in pages, and the pictures have to be put in their proper places along with their captions. By providing accurate and uncomplicated page layouts, you can save the printer time and yourself some money.

We have explained these matters of composition, makeup and press make-ready so that you can understand why the unit cost of a few thousand catalogs is high compared to that of many thousands. After the first investment in composition and make ready has been made, the cost per catalog drops rapidly as the number of those printed increases. The cost of composition and make-ready is practically the same for 10,000 catalogs as for 100,000. As your mailing list increases, your cost per catalog should drop.

The Printer Can Help

If you do not think you are equal to the task of preparing your own catalog, you can get help from an advertising agency. If you do, you supply the agency with the basic information, and its staff lays out the catalog and writes the copy. You can also obtain valuable assistance from catalog printers. Up-to-date printing houses maintain layout departments for their customers.

Do not try to cut costs by using cheap paper in your catalog. The savings will make little difference in the cost of the catalog, but it will make a big difference in appearance.

Some mail-order nursery businesses have been built without catalogs. These companies use newsapers and magazines to carry expensive advertising campaigns offering specific items. The usual practice is to offer only one item in each advertisement. Thus the advertiser may have several ads in a single issue of the newspaper or magazine. Readers are urged to order directly from the ads.

One innovative mail-order nurseryman bought several consecutive full pages of space in a popular garden magazine and used it to publish a mini-catalog, all in color.

There is a widespread impression that mail-order nursery stock is inferior to merchandise sold in local retail nurseries. Of course, this is erroneous.

BEGINNING IN THE NURSERY BUSINESS

True, some mail-order nurseries offer only poor stock at low prices, but they are the exceptions. Our advice is to build your business on good quality. Give customers high-grade merchandise and charge fair prices. You will be building your business on the soundest possible basis.

Do not worry about competitors who are underselling you. Price alone is a poor criterion for judging nursery stock. Poor stock that fails to grow or gives indifferent results is costly at any price. On the other hand, strong, healthy, well-graded plants can command good prices. There are plenty of people willing to pay fair prices for good stock.

Two Selling Policies

We want to relate the experiences of two successful mail-order nurseries. One sells small stock at low prices. The other offers only strong grades at much higher prices. Both have been operating for many years and cover much the same territory. Each mails out several hundred thousand catalogs every year.

The first company has such a big turnover among its customers that it must initiate an intensive advertising program every year to maintain its volume of business. The other nursery has been able to reduce its advertising budget materially without experiencing a drop in business. Its customers are so pleased that they buy year after year. They also tell their friends, who send in their own orders. These facts bear out the cliche, "A satisfied customer is the best advertisement."

Whether to require customers to prepay is a question you have to decide as part of your policy. If you cast about for advice, you can get all you want, pro and con. Both methods have strong advocates. We will attempt to present the arguments for both sides.

Large mail-order houses require prepayment for practically all of the nursery stock they offer. The reason is simple: It is difficult — in fact almost impossible — to estimate accurately the weight of nursery stock that is packed for shipment. So mail-order nurseries cannot tell their customers how much to include in their remittance for transportation. When all items are shipped prepaid, bookkeeping is simplified. It is not necessary to keep any records of postage, freight or express charges. When nursery stock is shipped prepaid, customers know exactly what their purchases cost when they are delivered.

Some leading mail-order nurseries that require prepayments now include a small charge on their order blanks with an explanatory note that it is for "packing and handling." This charge, no doubt, appears reasonable to customers, who pay it willingly.

Some mail-order nurseries require prepayments on all except a few specified items. The nurseries that do not usually charge their customers a reasonable percentage of the order's cost to cover transportation. These charges are presented to customers in a table.

You may be influenced somewhat by the practices of your competitors. If you are operating in a terrotory where most mail-order nurseries require prepayments, it may be the best policy for you to do the same.

Some mail-order nurseries have adopted a practice they refer to as a "pre-pruning service." Before they are shipped, plants are "partly pruned to bring roots and branches into proper balance. Thus when the plants arrive they are ready to set out." Of course, this also reduces the bulk and weight of the plants, thereby cutting the cost of packing and shipping.

One of your most difficult jobs will be pricing the items in your catalog. The usual tendency of beginners is to make prices too low. You must take into consideration all of the expenses involved in selling your products and getting them into the hands of the customers. In addition to the initial cost of the nursery stock, you must consider the expenses of advertising; printing and mailing catalogs; wrapping, packing and shipping orders; transportation (if you decide to require prepayments); and office overhead. Be sure you charge enough for your stock to cover these and all other expenses. And so that you have a reasonable margin of profit.

Guarantees

One of the problems you will encounter early in the game is that of formulating a guarantee. Customers want to know if you stand behind your products.

To make your position clear and to avoid misunderstandings with the customers, your catalog should state your policy in regard to guaranteeing nursery stock to grow. We believe that there is no more reason for guaranteeing nursery stock to grow than there is for guaranteeing that a shipment of baby chicks will survive or a package of cucumber seeds will germinate. If you send customers good stock that is well-packed, your responsibility should end there because you have no control over the shipments after they leave your hands. For all you know, the stock failed to grow because the package was left in the garage for two weeks or the family goat was pastured on it.

Regardless of your sentiments about guaranteeing nursery stock to grow, you are faced with the fact that it is a well-established custom among mail-order nurserymen to make some sort of guarantee.

Practically all guarantees begin with the reassuring statement that all plants are of first quality, true to name, and free of disease. Then follows a statement of what the nursery will do if the plants are not satisfactory. Here are some typical examples: (1) return the plants at once for free replacements, (2) return shipping labels within a specified time for free replacements or refunds, (3) report your loss by Aug. 1 for free replacements, (4) return orders at once for free replacements, or if anything planted fails to grow by Aug. 1 following shipment, it will be replaced free, (5) full guarantee up to 1 year or (6) unconditional guarantee.

These guarantees may seem so liberal that they could be costly. However, years of experience demonstrate that when orders are filled with good plants and packed carefully, the losses are minor. Furthermore, if you publish a guarantee and live up to it, you will have satisfied customers, who are your greatest assets.

The mail-order nursery business involves much detailed office work. This can be held to a minimum by planning office procedures carefully. Consider all the things that must be done to an order from the time it is received in your office until it has been filled. Outline the simplest and most logical procedure, and instruct your office workers to follow this outline in handling the orders. Such a plan will make for efficiency and accuracy.

Order Blanks

Your work is greatly simplified if you send order blanks to your customers when you mail them their catalogs. Of course, many people will not use them, but most buyers will. On each order blank provide spaces for all the information essential to handle the order efficiently. This includes the date, name, address, shipping station (if it is different from the post office), amount and form of money enclosed, quantity and varieties wanted, sizes, colors and prices. Also send an envelope with your name and address printed on it in large, clear type, and provide a space for the customer's return address. If you receive much mail other than mail order, a return envelope of a distinctive color or design will make it easier to separate mail orders from other mail.

Unless orders are to be shipped at once, acknowledge all of them promptly. Those orders are mighty important to the customers. They want to know if you have received them and when they will be shipped. Also, thank the customers for their business. Tell them how glad you are to have the opportunity to serve them. Make them think that you are really grateful. It costs so little to be courteous, yet it pays such big dividends. We find that the companies we like to do business with the most are usually the ones that are always pleased to get our orders, no matter how small they may be.

Tell customers that their orders will be shipped so that they arrive at the proper planting time. If some customers have specified shipment times, assure them that you will try to comply.

Often, especially toward the end of the selling season, you will run out of some varieties and will be tempted to substitute others to complete your orders. Our advice: do not do it without the customer's permission. Some nurseries provide a space on the order blanks asking their customers, "If a variety is not available, may we substitute one of equal or better value?"

When customers are entitled to refunds because they overpaid or because you cannot fill their orders completely, send the refunds promptly with letters or forms explaining why. It is good sales practice to suggest that perhaps they would like to use their checks to buy additional stock.

Often, customers fail to send enough money. Explain this to them and courteously request them to send the balance. It usually does not pay to hold up shipment of an order pending the payment of a balance due, especially if the amount is small. The majority of customers are honest and appreciate your confidence in them. Withholding shipment until a small balance is paid may cost you a good customer.

Keep a daily record of your sales to avoid the risk of overselling. The process of recording sales is known in the trade as collating, and the records are collates. Failure to keep sales records inevitably leads to trouble. Usually, you are surprised to discover that your stock of certain popular items is exhausted. By that time, it may be either too late or impossible to replenish your supply. Your customers will be disappointed and disgruntled, and you will have to refund a lot of money that you had already figured as part of your income.

Recording daily sales need not and should not be a complicated process. If your assortment is not too large, you can provide a place for every item on one or two big sheets. As these fill up, transfer the totals to another sheet that shows only the cumulative totals, the total sales to date. You should compare the total sales frequently with your record of stock reserved. When your supply of any items is exhausted, you can stop taking orders for it unless you know where you can get more at a price that leaves you a fair profit. These records also show you when the sales of any variety are lagging. This gives you a chance to protect yourself by trying to sell the surplus in other ways.

Inventory control can now be done by computer. A computer can be programmed to record your sales and make the information immediately available.

Some mail-order nurseries fill orders directly from the original order forms without copying them. This may not be a good practice. Anyone who has seen large numbers of mail orders knows how illegible and inaccurate they often are. It is better to copy the orders onto specially prepared forms. This work can be made easier by having all the varieties and grades you offer printed on the form. You should also provide places for essential information, such as the name, address, order number and manner of shipment. This printed

MAIL-ORDER NURSERIES

form can be sent to the customer with the order, serving as a type of invoice.

Mail-order nurserymen, like all other nurserymen, must be licensed to do business. Every state has a licensing bureau, which is usually part of the state department of agriculture or of the state agricultural college. If you grow your own nursery stock, it must be inspected. If it is given a clean bill of health, you will be issued a certificate of inspection. To nurserymen who buy all of their stock, a dealer's certificate is issued. Usually, a small fee is charged for the inspection service or for issuing a dealer's certificate. A copy of your certificate must appear on every package of stock you send out.

Vast improvements have been made in recent years in the methods of packing nursery stock for shipping. Polyethylene film has largely replaced heavy, wet packing materials around the roots. With this film, nursery stock arrives in better condition and weighs less, resulting in big savings in transportation expenses. You should inform yourself on these modern methods of packing so that you can benefit fully from them.

Every customer should be provided with planting instructions. The average planter knows little about planting and caring for plants. The more completely informed customers become on the subject, the better results they will have with your nursery stock.

You are bound to receive some complaints. Give them prompt and courteous attention. A few customers will try to take advantage of you, but the number is so small that it is almost negligible. A courteous letter responding to each complaint by expressing regret and showing a genuine interest in the matter more often than not dispels the customer's anger. Above all, do not refer to your "policy." Customers are not interested in it; they want to know specifically what you are going to do for them.

Sometimes it will be in your best interest to forget all about the terms of your guarantee and go all the way in making free replacements. This is especially true if the customers involved are of long standing.

When you make a replacement under such circumstances, do it graciously, Conceal from the customers any feelings of resentment you may have. They do not have to buy from you. Often it is cheaper to keep old customers than it is to go out and find new ones.

It has been mentioned that some mail-order nurseries are issuing fall catalogs. Until recently, the selling season for mail-order nurseries has been confined almost entirely to January through May. In most sections of the country, fall planting is satisfactory and, in fact, preferred to spring. However, this has not been generally recognized by the public. The knowledge that "Fall Is for Planting" is spreading across the country. It is likely that fall planting will greatly increase, thereby justifying mail-order nurserymen in issuing more fall nursery catalogs.

There is a strong organization of mail-order nurserymen, known as the Mailorder Association of Nurserymen Inc. Membership in this group should be of inestimable value.

Chapter 6.
Container-Grown Nursery Stock

Container-Grown Nursery Stock

Container-grown nursery stock is such an important part of the nursery industry that we are discussing it in a separate chapter. It has brought about what is probably the most important change in nursery stock retailing that the industry has ever experienced.

There is an important difference between container-grown and potted plants. This difference should be understood. Container-grown plants ae those that have been grown entirely in containers. At no time have they been cultivated in a field. Small starting plants are planted into containers and remain in them until they are ready to be sold.

Potted stock is defined as nursery stock that has been grown in the field and then transplanted into some sort of container. Several receptacles are used — tin cans, asphaltpaper pots, baskets, papier-mache and clay pots, and wooden boxes or tubs. Rosebushes are a good example of plants that are grown in the field but are commonly transplanted while they are dormant to pots for retail marketing.

A full understanding of the role that container-grown plants play in today's nursery stock marketing demands a history review. Container growing cannot be called a new practice because woodcuts in books published hundreds of years ago show workers transplanting plants into the garden from pots. However, commercial production in this country began only 50 or 60 years ago in California.

Using plants grown in containers moved slowly eastward through Arizona, New Mexico and into Texas. It was practiced almost entirely in these Southern states. The containers were mostly used 1-gallon fruit cans. Many still had pieces of labels attached to them, others were rusty or dented. The retail nurserymen who sold these container-grown plants usually placed them on the ground under shade. They rarely make attractive displays. Often, such nurseries were referred to as "tin-can nurseries" in derision.

Eventually, the cans were treated with a black, waterproofing preparation that greatly improved their appearances. Larger cans were also used — ones that had once contained eggs or lard for bakers, for example. Because all these cans had straight sides, it was difficult or nearly impossible to remove the plants without first cutting the cans from top to bottom on opposite sides. The sides were then spread apart, and the plants could be removed.

A special can cutter was invented for this purpose. It had long handles so that nurserymen could do the cutting while standing. Handling cut cans sometimes caused bad cuts on fingers and wrists. If, after being cut, the cans were to be taken away by customers, the sides had to be tied together again with wire or cord. The straight-sided can was far from satisfactory.

The problem was solved with the introduction of cans with sides tapered like those of ordinary clay pots. Plants could be easily removed from these pots without having to cut the containers. Today, almost all containers are tapered.

With better-quality plants and aggressive marketing practices, California nurserymen began to develop markets in the East and North. Today, contaienr-grown plants ae produced and sold in all sections of the country. They represent a rapidly increasing percentage of all the nursery stock produced.

It is fair to ask why container-grown nursery stock is enjoying such a wide acceptance. What are its advantages? One reason is that nurserymen can grow many more plants in a given area in containers than they can in the field. For example, one acre of ground holds more than 90,000 plants in the so-called 1-gallon cans, even after half of the area is set aside for walks and service drives. This is several times the number of plants that could be placed in the same area under normal field culture.

When large numbers of plants are concentrated in a small area, it is easier and more economical to control the applications of water and fertilizer. Less weeding is necessary. Spraying, dusting and pruning can be done more readily.

Growing nursery stock in containers usually results in a much higher percentage of marketable plants than is possible by growing in the field. It is not unusual for nurserymen to put 90 percent of the plants they originally planted in cans on the market. Experienced nurserymen know that this is a far greater percentage of marketable plants than they can hope to obtain with field-grown stock.

These advantages of container-grown plants are of special interest to the growers. But what about the retailers, the people who sell this stock to the consumers? We have already said that container-grown stock has brought about what are probably the most important changes in retailing nursery material. To understand this, a little more history on the early days of garden centers is needed.

After World War II, garden centers were being opened all over the country. This was before container-grown plants were accepted, or even available. Most nursery stock was sold bare root. Evergreens and large shade trees were dug with balls of earth around their roots. But all fruit trees, shrubs, hedge plants, grape vines — indeed, all deciduous plants — were sold bare root. To keep these plants in good condition nurserymen stood them in beds with moist packing material around their roots. Very few garden centers had buildings in which these plants could be displayed. Nearly all nursery stock was displayed outdoors.

When a customer bought a bare root plant, it had to be pulled out of the bed, thereby disturbing the packing around the other plants. The packing had to be put back in place — if it was not overlooked. Then the purchased plant had to be taken indoors so that its roots could be wrapped with moist packing material. If the plant was bought on Saturday, the customer probably intended to set it out that afternoon or on Sunday. But if the weather was ideal for golf or fishing, the plant would have to wait — and did, probably without having any water added to the packing. The performance of the plant when eventually set out may not have been good and was not the fault of the nurseryman.

As the buds began to swell on the plants in the beds, the chances of successful establishment decreased rapidly. Selling these bare-root plants had to stop altogether, and the selling season was over. Some years, this was a very short time indeed. What did garden centers do with these unsold plants? If there was room, the plants were set out in nursery rows and cared for all summer. This was not a very satisfactory practice, but the alternative was to burn them. In fact, stock was often burned — a severe loss!

During this period, another practice was developing. Rosebushes, shrubs, small shade ornamentals and fruit trees were being root-wrapped and offered for sale inside the garden store. These were ready for impulse buyers. Nice days early in the season brought out enthusiastic gardeners ready to buy some plants. This gambit worked quite well. Today, of course, it is a universal practice. especially of mass marketers.

It is still the practice of some garden centers today to offer an assortment of bare-root plants, partly because they can be sold for a little less and partly because some gardeners prefer them. However, by far the greater portion of nursery stock sold today in garden centers is sold in containers of some sort. It is either container-grown, potted, B&B

or put in baskets or boxes.

Such stock is ready for customers to take home as soon as they buy it. It requires no wrapping or can cutting. If golf, fishing or other diversions delay planting for a few days — or even a week or longer if the soil is watered — the chances of container-grown plants surviving are good. Container-grown material gives better results than do bare-root plants because its roots are already active.

Container-grown nursery stock allows customers to acquire plants whenever they get the notion. Often, customers have no desire to buy certain plants until they see them in bloom in neighbors' yards or in parks. By that time, it is too late to sell bare-root plants, and nurserymen have lost sales. But if the plants are available in containers, the customers can satisfy their desires at once, and the nurserymen have made more sales.

In garden centers, customers often buy plants that they had no intention of buying when they came in. This is known as impulse buying. The plants appeal in some way to the customers, and the sales are made merely because the plants were prominently displayed. It is easy to make attractive displays of container-grown nursery stock in various places in the nursery or garden center, thereby encouraging impulse buying. Container-grown nursery stock is ready for sale at any time. When customers make up their minds to buy certain plants, all they have to do is pick them up (if they are not too heavy) and take them to a salesman or the cashier. Displaying such plants encourages self-service.

Attractive displays are an esesential part of good merchandising. Container-grown nursery stock lends itself readily to display, especially when the containers are of uniform size, clean and free from rust. Containers help dress up the plants, showing them off to their best advantage. No special facilities are needed to build an attention-getting display. Because the plants are easily moved, it is no trouble to change the displays at frequent intervals. Displays can readily be kept complete. When one plant is sold, another can be moved in from the reserve stock.

For some reason, customers have more faith in the condition of plants that have their roots already established in soil. There is less resistance to buying container plants in a dormant state than there is to buying dormant bare-root plants. Sales of container-grown plants increase rapidly when the plants start to grow. When transplanted carefully into the customers' gardens, they keep growing.

Container-grown nursery stock usually gives customers better results than they get from dormant bare-root stock. Losses are fewer because there is little shock in transplanting. This not only makes the customers happy but the nurserymen as well, because they receive fewer complaints.

Retailers also get better results from container-grown nursery stock. They lose fewer plants waiting to be sold. It is also easier to keep these plants in good condition. Any plants left on hand at the end of the selling season can be carried over to the next season.

Perhaps the greatest advantage of selling container-grown stock is that it extends the planting season. It is ready for sale at all times and can be transplanted any time people can dig in the ground. Sales may be made during any month in the South. With container-grown plants, retailers do not need to wait until the plants become dormant to sell them.

In the Northern states, the planting season can be extended through summer and into fall. Dormant bare-root nursery stock cannot be transplanted safely after it starts to grow. This limits its sale to the time when it is dormant and the ground is not frozen — a few weeks in fall and a few weeks in spring.

The selling season for container-grown nursery stock begins as soon as the frost is gone in spring and continues until the ground freezes in fall or winter. It is true that the urge to plant often dwindles with the advent of hot sumemr weather, but the gadening public is gradually learning that container-grown stock can be planted successfully all summer. In areas where the public has become accustomed to container-grown stock, summer sales continue to increase.

Growing stock in containers had disadvantages for producers. Because of the limited capacity of the cans, plants become pot-bound if they remain in them too long before being transplanted or sold. The term, pot-bound, means that a plant's roots have completely filled the available space in the can and have nowhere else to go. Such plants are likely to be seriously stunted when they are transplanted.

Growers of container-grown nursery stock must plan their production schedules so that they can dispose of their plants before they become pot-bound, or they should arrange to transplant them into larger containers. In actual practice, it is difficult to schedule production to avoid all unplanned repotting.

Unlike the early days of the container industry, when the only cans available were those previously used for fruit, cooking oil, eggs and the like, or other kinds of cans, the industry today is flooded with containers of many sizes, shapes and materials. Cans can be made of metal, fiber or plastic and are round, hexagonal or square. They range in capacity from 1 to 20 gallons. Besides all of these, there are polyethylene bags.

Today, the most widely used containers are round, made of metal and have capacities of 1, 2 and 5 gallons. There is an increasing use of large cans for growing the larger plants needed in landscape plantings. The advantages of hexagonal and square containers, their manufacturers point out, is that they fit closer together, thereby savings space. The manufacturers also claim that the plants, being so close together, are afforded better protection in winter.

There is a limited use of polyethylene bags for container growing. They were used almost exclusively in England when the industry began and are still widely used there. They are less expensive than cans and take less space to store. They are strong enough for the job but hard to fill. A recent survey in England revealed that the use of polyethylene bags is waning. Rigid containers are being more widely used.

In the early days of container-grown stock production, the containers were placed on the ground and filled by hand. Then the containers were placed on benches and the small plants to be grown were planted in them. All of this was a slow, tedious and costly process. Before many years passed, machines were built to fill the pots and set the plants in one continuous process.

A problem that confronts most large-scale producers of container-grown plants is choosing the growing medium to fill the containers. At first, producers believed that fertile topsoil was required, but it is rarely available in large volumes. Substitutes had to be found, and the search for the best and most economical mix is still going on.

At present, the following materials are among those in use: topsoil, subsoil, sand, sedge, peat, decayed bark, composted sawdust, shavings and cottonseed hulls. All are used in varying combinations and proportions.

The mix anchors the plants, and supplies them with water and nourishment. Obviously, some mix materials contain little or no plant food. Consequently, some mixes need more fertilizer than others. Furthermore, a mix must have a reasonably good water-holding capacity. These are problems that growers must solve for themselves.

How the growers solve these problems is of vital concern to the retailer, who probably know nothing about the fertility or water-holding capacity of the container mixes they buy. They know they have to water the plants, but what about feeding them? Is it necessary while the plants are on sale?

Some growers, mindful of the problems facing the customers, are trying to do something about them. They are adding long-lasting, slow-release fertilizers to their container mixes. To give the mixes greater moisture-holding capacities, they are also adding more organic materials. Such practices could make it needless for retailers to feed their plants while they are up for sale and reduce the need for watering. By using chemical weed killers, growers can also keep the containers free of weeds.

Because of the weight and bulk of container-grown plants, the only economical way to ship them to retailers is by contract truck haulers. If a customer's order does not fill a truck, other orders for the same area can be combined with it to make a full truckload.

For many years after their introduction, container-grown plants were listed and sold by the capacities of their containers. The size of the plants were not indicated. Plant size had to be assumed by the retailers. If, from experience, they knew that a certain variety of plant in a 1-gallon container produced by a certain grower was usually of a certain size, they assumed that the same variety would be the same size in subsequent orders.

This is a very unsatisfactory practice for the retailers. For example, a landscape nurseryman needs 100 'Pfitzeriana' junipers 2 to 2½ feet in diameter. From past experience, he has learned that these usually come in 5-gallon containers. Accordingly, he orders that size. When they come, a number are considerably smaller than 2 to 2½ feet. This creates a problem. It is useless to complain because his order was filled with plants in 5-gallon containers.

Dissatisfaction with this way of selling container-grown plants became so general that the nursery industry realized that something would have to be done. Could any old-time nurserymen ever have dreamed that nursery stock would someday be sold by the gallon?

A number of growers began to list plant sizes as well as container capacities. However, this did not become a general practice — many growers would not go along with it. Eventually, the problem was turned over to the Horticultural Standards Committee of the American Association of Nurserymen. Standards for all other major classes of nursery stock had been established long ago and were accepted and used by the nursery industry.

The committee worked long and diligently to come up with standards for the products of the container industry. These standards are comprehensive and are now a part of the "American Standards for Nursery Stock." Because they are extensive and detailed, we shall not attempt to explain them. We are glad, however, to report that it is now the general practice in the industry to list the size of the plant as well as that of the container. Unfortunately, a few growers are still holding out.

Chapter 7. Interior Landscaping

Interior Landscaping

The most recent addition to the businesses that make up the nursery industry is the one that creates landscapes indoors. As with most newborns, there was considerable discussion about what to name this infant industry. "Interior plantscaping," "interior landscaping" and merely "plantscaping" were among the suggestions. The one that seems to be most widely accepted today is "interior landscaping," although many others in the business still prefer "interior plantscaping."

The business is so new that its entire development has occurred during the past 20 years, yet its growth has been so rapid that it has become a multimillion dollar business that is flourishing in all sections of the country. This suggests that there is a widespread need for it and that the need is being fulfilled.

What is interior landscaping? In the simplest terms, it consists of bringing plants indoors to simulate creations of Mother Nature. It might consist of using only a few plants to decorate the entrance of a building, or it could be designing an extensive landscape comprising many hundreds, even thousands, of plants.

What is the purpose of bringing plants indoors? Indoors is not their natural habitat — why put them there? The reasons are numerous and vary somewhat, depending upon the function of the building in which they are installed.

In past years, the grounds around factory buildings and warehouses were usually unkempt and unattractive. When one such site was cleaned up, the workers took pride in its appearance and had better attitudes toward their work. This effect was especially true if the grounds were landscaped. Today, one rarely sees a factory or warehouse the grounds of which are not neat and clean or without some degree of landscaping. The owners would not be doing this if it were not a good investment.

If landscaping causes such favorable reactions among employees in the factory, why would bringing the landscape indoors not have a similar effect? From the very beginning, this has proved to be true. Landscaping the interior of a large office brings in a bit of nature and relaxes the workers, making them happier and more efficient. It also demonstrates that the employer cares.

Landscaping in a shopping mall has a tendency to slow the traffic. Shoppers feel more leisurely and are likely to take more time shopping. In apartment complexes, strategically placed plantings give the residents a feeling of comfort — a sense of being at home. In a bank, a well-planned plant arrangement puts customers at ease. It might even dull the pain of 15 percent interest on their loans! There are many other public and semipublic buildings where landscape plantings can be found.

Many luxury hotels across the country have installed elaboerate interior landscapes. To cite only one example: A large, elegant Midwestern hotel has a big, beautiful, hillside garden at one end of the lobby, complete with trees, shrubs, flowers and running water. An ornamental stairway angles up through the garden, affording visitors many entrancing views. The purpose of the landscape is to increase the patrons' enjoyment and to generate goodwill.

There are many other reasons for interior landscaping. If a common denominator were to be found for the existence of all the interior landscapes, it probably would be the nearly universal love of nature. Bringing plants indoors and arranging them in a pleasing manner help satisfy this love. Plants have a soothing influence.

The origin of the practice of bringing plants indoors for decorative purposes is not new. In Victorian days, large pots of palms and Boston ferns could be seen through the big front windows of many homes. Many hotels in big cities in those days had long "peacock alleys" lined with potted palms. Palms were used to conceal quiet corners and were used liberally to decorate the lobby.

The business of interior landscaping has grown very rapidly. It is estimated that its practitioners now number in the thousands. The competition is severe, and there are bound to be numerous failures. It is not difficult to get into the business, but staying there requires many things. There is so much interior landscapers need to know about plants and their care that many in practice now are not qualified.

Perhaps the best place to enter the interior landscape business is near large cities. Up to the present time, most buyers of interior landscapes have been businesses in large cities. They are the ones most in need of it and are probably the best able to afford it. However, some observers believe that good markets in smaller towns are being overlooked. There is also less competition there. Numerous potential interior landscape customers have not been mentioned. Among them are churches, clubhouses, lodges, large homes, shopping centers, rest homes, courthouses and auditoriums.

The plants used in outdoor landscaping cannot be used for creating interior landscapes. These outdoor plants of the temperate zone are conditioned to extreme changes in weather. In autumn, they lose foliage and become dormant. They would survive only a short time indoors.

For interior landscaping, plants that remain green year-around and that do not become dormant are needed. This means tropical plants. Accordingly, tropical plants are used almost exclusively in indoor landscapes.

Unless you are already familiar with many tropical plants when you decide to become a part of the interior landscape business, you have to become acquainted with a wide range of them. You need to know how large and how rapidly they grow, what shapes they assume, the texture of their foliage and much, much more.

As with outdoor landscapes, plans have to be prepared for indoor landscapes. Usually, this is the function of the designer who draws the plans for the entire project. If the indoor garden is to be in a building that is still in the planning stage, the ideal arrangement would be for the designer to cooperate with the building architect, who may not be familiar with all the requirements of an interior landscape.

The areas to be landscaped must have sufficient light for the plants to thrive. Changes might have to be made in its floor plan to accommodate the plants so that they will not interfere with the primary use of the room. Provision needs to be made for the plants' light requirements, either natural or artificial. A further problem is that of adequate shade and light. The plants selected by the contractor may not thrive under the conditions in which they are placed.

Facilities for watering must be conveniently located. Plants must not be exposed to moving, heated air. If the architect and designer work out these problems together, they can avoid many later troubles.

This arrangement is ideal only if the designer is fully informed on all phases of plant design, as well as on the plants needed to execute the design and the care of those plants. Unfortunately, there are designers who can create a pleasing scene in outline but are incapable of specifying the plants to be used to execute their plans. This poses serious problems for the people who have to carry out their designs.

For example, a design might specify a slender plant about 6 feet tall with a rounded head. Or the plan might require a low-spreading, flowering plant. What do you use? Obviously, plans executed in this fashion cannot have

INTERIOR LANDSCAPING

the uniformity and cohesiveness of a plan that gives complete specifications.

The failure of a designer to give complete specifications causes serious problems for the contractor. The owner may not like some of the plants chosen, or the sizes may not be suitable. The texture of some of the plants may clash, and so on.

Some contractors do their own planning, thereby taking responsibility for the entire job. They may have had experience in designing outdoor landscapes — the principles are the same. Such contractors are often in the garden center business, have engaged in landscaping and sell tropical plants in their garden centers.

When an interior landscape has been completed, its requirements are not completely fulfilled. It has to be maintained. The question always arises: Who is going to do it? Maintenance could be done by the owner or the contractor who installed it. A third option is to turn the job over to professionals whose business it is to maintain indoor landscapes. These companies are primarily interested in working with large projects.

Maintaining an interior landscape is not a simple matter. It calls for many essential practices that require specific knowledge and skill. The question of who is to be responsible for the care of an interior landscape is one that should be determined even before the project is started.

Before we discuss the needs of the plants, you need to have an understanding of the nature of the plants. It has already been explained that only tropical plants are used in interior landscapes. Most are produced in the southernmost areas of the US outdoors in full sun. Before they can be used indoors, these plants must be acclimatized, which the growers do before shipping the plants to the customers.

They acclimatize their plants by reducing the light to which they are exposed, usually with some form of shade. Small plants can be placed in the shade of larger ones, but taller plants need varying degrees of overhead shade. The time required varies according to the type of plant and to its size. The purpose of this process is to adjust the plants to the reduced light to which they will be subjected when they become part of an interior landscape.

The proper care of these tropical plants calls for many different practices. The most obvious, of course, is watering and fertilizing. Plants have varying light requirements, and they do not do well unless these needs are met. Light meters are used to measure the light, which is expressed in footcandles. Specific temperature requirements must be met if the plants are to survive and remain healthy. This is complicated at times by the practice, in some buildings, of reducing the heat at night.

From time to time, the foliage needs cleaning. Pruning and shearing may also be required. Unhappily, diseases and injurious insects are sometimes encountered.

The care of an interior landscape can be met in three ways. It can be the responsibility of the contractor who installed it, the owner or a professional maintenance company. Whoever chooses to do the job must be reasonably well qualified to perform the tasks listed above. The contractor is most likely to do the work well, especialy if he has had more than a little experience. It is not likely that many owners would be able to do the work properly; neither is it likely that many would want to do it unless the planting was small.

The third option is to use professionals. Companies that specialize in caring for interior landscapes contract with owners to keep their plantings in prime condition. Employees of these companies have been trained to perform the various tasks required. These caretaker companies are a great boon to the interior landscape business, whose creations might otherwise suffer for lack of proper care.

Interior landscaping is a new business and is faced with numerous problems, as is any new enterprise. Perhaps the most serious is that of vague designs. Interior landscape contractors complain that too often the plans made by designers lack detail. They do not specify the plants to be used. They fail to indicate the intensity of the light available. Often the only clues the contractor has concerning the plants to be used are the shapes or outlines of the plants indicated in the design.

Such plans place too much responsibility on the contractor and make it very difficult to select the plants that will produce the most attractive landscape. The designer should provide all the details the planter needs, including the plants to use and their light, temperature and mositure requirements.

The nurserymen who grow the tropical plants required for interior landscapes have done a good job producing them, especially when you condider the newness of the business. They have made available a very fine assortment of plants, which makes possible a wide array of designs.

Some designers and contractors think there is a need for a wider range of plants. There are nurserymen who are trying to fill this need. Some complain, however, that when they introduce new plants that they know can be useful, they are unable to sell them. The designer's or conrtractor's reaction is, "Let someone else try it first." The nursery industry has had to contend with this attitude for a long time.

The burgeoning of the interior landscape business has been a boon to the tropical plant industry because it has created a new market for its products. Many growers have expanded their businesses. Others have been encouraged to enter the industry. A corollary to all this is that supermarkewts and discount houses have generated an additional market for foliage plants.

Nurserymen experienced in the interior landscape business have learned the importance of a written contract between client and contractor. So many exigencies are involved in this business that misunderstandings can easily develop. It is important to have all angles of a job specified in a contract — to include every facet that you can think of, especially all costs. Pricing is the element that probably is the most difficult. The costs of materials, labor, services and the like are difficult to figure, but they must be considered.

It is not difficult to get started in the interior landscape business, and the ease of doing so has caused malpractices by inexperienced contractors that have been disservices to the clients. There is a need for more professionalism in the industry. This includes an appreciation for design and wide-ranging acquaintence with tropical plants for interior use, their needs and how fo fulfill them.

The interior landscape business is well-organized. There are two national associations: Inrterior Plantscape Association and the Interior Landscape division of the Associated Landscape Contractors of America.

The latter has undertaken the task of setting standards for the industry, which have been published in a handbook called "Guide to Specifications for Interior Landscaping." Already accepted as the standard for the industry, this text covers a wide range of concerns, including specifications for individual plants, lighting requirements, pot sizes, specifications for soil mix and light parameters. It also illustrates, in color, 56 plants for interior use. An important feature is a detailed discussion of contractual, installation and maintenance practices.

Chapter 8. Wholesale Nurseries

Wholesale Nurseries

Wholesale nurseries, sometimes called wholesale growers, produce nursery stock for retail nurseries, garden centers, landscape nurseries and mail-order nurseries.

Wholesale nurseries are well-distributed across the country and supply the needs of retailers. Many are more than 100 years old and are family-owned operations that have been passed from one generation to another. There is a tremendous variation in the sizes of wholesale nurseries. Some cover 2,000 acres or more, while others may occupy only a few acres.

The operation's size depends primarily on the plants it produces. Large nurseries usually grow complete assortments of plants needed by retailers. There are, however, some large nurseries that produce only one class of plants — for example, roses or fruit trees. Another factor that governs the size of a nursery is the method of production. As a rule, more container-grown plants can be grown on an acre than can field-grown plants of the same size.

Small wholesale nurseries specialize, growing only classes of plants, such as rhododendrons and azaleas, ground covers and vines, perennials, small fruits or lining-out stock.

Some large wholesale nurseries in the US grow as many as 1,000 different kinds of plants. They attempt to supply all the needs of the retailers. Interestingly, Hilliers and Sons, a fifth-generation nursery in Winchester, England, cultivates about 14,000 different kinds of plants. Of these, 8,000 are listed in Hillier's Catalog. Without a doubt, this is the greatest hardy tree and shrub nursery in the world.

The location of a wholesale nursery depends upon a number of considerations. Some nurseries are in their present locations purely by chance. Perhaps the owners lived in certain areas and wanted to stay there so that is where their nurseries are located despite the advantages or disadvantages.

The better markets for wholesale sales are, of course, in the metropolitan areas where there is the greatest concentration of people. The disadvantage of such a location is the high cost of land. High taxes could easily erode profits. Nurserymen have to weigh the advantage of a good market against the cost of the land. As a rule, it is not profitable to grow nursery stock on high-priced land.

Different classes of plants require various types of soil. If you want to produce evergreens to be dug with a ball of earth, the soil must have a high clay content. Good balls cannot be made with loose, sandy soil. If you want a general assortment of nursery stock, you must decide which soil type to use depending upon the requirements of the more important plants to be produced — those that will generate the most income.

Some wholesale nurseries are located a great distance from their markets. The sites were chosen because they offered soil of superior quality. The lower cost of production on such soils offsets the additional cost of getting the plants to market.

Water is another factor that may merit attention. If your nursery is in an area that depends on irrigation, you must be certain that the necessary water is available.

If the nursery is to be used to produce container-grown plants, there are special factors to be considered. The land needs to be fairly level. Some gentle slopes are acceptable, but steep slopes can lead to serious erosion. The availability of water is of prime importance. Water is required not only to assuage the plants' thirst but also to apply plant food.

Most important of all is the potential supply of soil needed to fill the containers. Nurserymen who are not familiar with the practice might be astonished

BEGINNING IN THE NURSERY BUSINESS

at the amount of soil it requires. Topsoil is preferred, but today other ingredients are sometimes mixed with it. Among them are well-rotted tree bark and nitrogen-fortified, composted shavings or sawdust. Some nurseries add a slow-release nutrient to their mixes.

At this point, we should point out the difference between container-grown plants and potted stock. Unlike container-grown plants, which spend their entire lives in containers, potted plants are field-grown stock that are transplanted to containers. There is a further distinction: Some potted plants are dug from the field with soil around the roots and placed in pots. Others are dug bare root and planted in pots with soil or a compost of some kind. These plants may be potted in fall and placed in polyethylene-covered houses or sheds over winter without heat, while others may be dug in the field and potted in early spring.

It is a standard practice to transplant field-grown rosebushes into pots in fall or as soon as they are dormant. Quite often, they are kept over winter in poly houses or under other shelter where enough heat can be applied to encourage early root growth. These roses are ready to take off, grow and bloom soon after they are set out for sale in spring. It is likely that the great majority of roses sold in spring have been handled in this fashion.

After you have chosen the location of your wholesale nursery, you must decide what to grow. This depends on the markets you are targeting — those you want to reach. Garden centers usually offer a general assortment of plants, mostly in sizes that can be taken home in the family car. Landscape nurseries are important customers that usually need larger trees, shrubs and evergreens for immediate effect. The needs of these two markets overlap considerably. Consequently, wholesalers can readily take care of both.

Not all mail-order nurseries grow their own plants. Those that do not are potential customers. As a rule, many plants sold by mail-order nurseries are smaller than those offered by garden centers. This is not to say that they are of inferior quality — not at all! However, smaller plants are bound to hold down the cost of transportation. Most mail-order nurseries today offer wider plant assortments than do many garden centers because many retailers have limited display space.

The following is a list of nursery stock categories for any wholesale nursery that plans to produce a general line: shade, ornamental and flowering trees; conifers; broad-leaved evergreens; flowering shrubs; roses; ground covers; hedge plants; vines; fruit trees; small fruits; and perennials.

It is important to grow only plants that are hardy in the area you plan to serve. You can get much information on selecting plant assortments by visiting garden centers in your area. A study of mail-order catalogs would be helpful and so will a careful perusal of the catalogs offered by wholesale nurseries serving the area. You can get more help from the horticulture departments of state universities. The ultimate choices will depend on the experiences of others in your area.

Reproducing the plants you have chosen to grow so that they reach salable sizes involves some of the industry's most highly skilled individuals — plant propagators. Plant propagation is a process that is as much art as it is science.

Because of the great variety of plants, many different methods are used to propagate them. The most common follow.

• Hardwood cuttings are planted directly in the field.
• Softwood cuttings are rooted in greenhouses or outdoor beds and subjected to frequently applied mist.
• Seeds are planted directly in the

field or in beds. They can be used outdoors or in greenhouses.

• Grafts involve dormant scions on dormant, bare-root seedlings, or growing scions on young but established and growing potted plants.

• T-Budding is mostly a field practice. It involves slipping a dormant bud into a T-shaped slit in the bark of an understock plant. The bud ends up next to the cambium of the host stock.

These propagation methods have been used for centuries, but some new ones have recently evolved. Among these is micropropagation or tissue culture, perhaps better known as "cloning."

Tissue culture has both good and bad points. It is expensive but allows a nurseryman to produce thousands of new plants, each of which is nearly identical to the single, superior parent. To produce these plants, a technician removes, under aseptic (germ-free) conditions, a tiny amount of meristematic (undifferentiated) tissue from the growing point of a selected parent plant. This tissue is surface sterilized in a series of baths, the first of which contains a dilute disinfectant, while the others are sterile, distilled water.

The tissue is then removed and deftly placed on a special, solid medium in a sterile vessel, usually a plastic bottle made for the purpose or a common, glass prescription bottle. Prescription bottles are equipped with plastic screwcaps; they can, therefore, be kept free of contaminants, including airborne fungi and bacteria as well as mites, which could otherwise simply walk in. The medium contains a mixture of hormones, vitamins and nutrients.

The vessels are put on racks in a "clean" room, where the entering air is filtered, and the light, temperature and relative humidity levels can be rigidly controlled, monitored and recorded. Developing tissues are continually transfered, under asceptic conditions, to new bottles containing specific amounts of inorganic salts and other critical ingredients (2,4-D often being one). By manipulating the physical environment, a technician can watch what appears, at first, to be thousands of amorphous, washed-out, green blobs of callus tissue become new plants (called explants), which are miniature versions of their parents.

These new plants are removed, potted and prepared for the field by methods similar to those used to acclimatize tropical plants intended for interior landscapes.

Two singular disadvantages of tissue culture are its relatively high cost and the frequently alarming mortality rate observed when the young explants are transferred from their near-optimum laboratory environment to the much harsher one found in the field. There have been some claims — largely premature ones — that this problem has been solved. Unfortunately, it has not; but intensive study of the problem is being done now. This will surely yield some answers. Changing the intensity and quality of the light to which the explants are subjected while they are developing has produced some encouraging results.

The high cost per unit of micropropagated plants results directly from the considerable expense of starting a laboratory and the need for technologists with laboratory experience, enduring patience, superior manual dexterity and thorough knowledge of aseptic techniques. It also takes a relatively long time to convert a warren of undifferentiated cells into "hardened-off", recognizable plants capable of surviving in the field.

Despite these disadvantages, tissue culture will likely become the wave of the future in plant propagation and will inevitably lead to the development and introduction of many new and better plants.

This art of plant propagation is so varied and complicated that it cannot be presented satisfactorily in terms easy to understand. It is developing so rapidly that there is now an international association of plant propagators with separate chapters in every part of the world.

If you plan to grow nursery stock for the wholesale trade, the least expensive way to get started is to buy the small plants you need and put them in the field to grow. These plants are known as lining-out stock, and the trade description for them is LOS. There are companies that make a business of producing LOS for the trade. Because of the great variety of plants needed, there is no one source for the necessary LOS. You have to buy it from several, possibly many, sources.

Another problem facing the beginner in the business is deciding how many plants to grow. There is no easy answer because there is no way to forecast how many plants of each variety plants you will be able to sell. The information you gather when deciding what varieties to grow affords a clue to the popularity of various kinds of plants. This information should be helpful in deciding how many of each to grow. The best advice is to be conservative.

Then another problem presents itself. How long should these plants be left in the field? How large should they be before they are offered for sale? The ultimate answers to those questions have to depend on experience. As a rule, garden centers use plants somewhat smaller than those used by landscapers.

There is a great variation in plant growth rates. Some plants grow so rapidly they can be harvested at the end of one growing season. Others require several years of growth before they are marketable. For this reason, slower growing plants are best planted in an area separate from faster growing ones. Some plants are grown in the open field. Others can be grown in beds or close rows. There is a wide variation in the practices used in growing plants to marketable sizes.

The nurseries from which you buy your LOS can be helpful in advising you how best to handle it in the field. Perhaps the most practical way to learn about field practices is to visit several nurseries with camera and notebook. Nurserymen are a friendly lot and are willing to share their know-how with others, especially with those who share their interest, a love of plants.

After planting the LOS, you must observe other practices, such as cultivating, pruning and pest control. It is not practical to go into detail on these practices, but you must be prepared for them.

Keep in mind that as long as a plant remains in the ground in the field, the cost of caring for it continues. This means that plants in the field are an investment of money without any return. Accordingly, the longer a plant stays in the ground, the greater your investment in it is. You can be reasonably certain that there will be a market for such plants at prices that will cover all your costs and ensure you of reasonable profits.

However, accurately determining the cost of producing a specific plant is nearly impossible, unless you are producing only a very limited assortment. For example, a small shrub may be in a block alongside a block of shade trees that are 5 or 6 yers old. The two blocks are cultivated at the same time, but it is unlikely that the cost of each block is recorded or charged against each one. The same is true of the cost of fertilizing, pruning and other cultural practices that have to be done to both blocks.

The field practices of the nursery industry have been greatly improved during recent years. Not too many years ago, every graft, cutting and seedling had to be set out in the field by hand. Much of the cultivating was done by hand with hoes. If plants were to be set out in beds, the beds had to be made by hand using shovels and rakes. When plants had to be sprayed for diseases and insects, it was probably done by hand. The spraying equipment was carried on the workers' backs.

Nurserymen in business today can remember the time when most nursery stock was dug by hand. Two men, one on each side of the row, had heavy, ironbound shaft handle spades that they forced into the ground. By prying and lifting, they could remove the plants from the ground; it was hard, hard work. As was to be expected, however, the roots were often quite short. The story is told of one nurseryman who, upon receiving a shipment of short-rooted fruit trees, wired the shipper, "Trees received. Please send roots."

Today, the picture has changed dramatically. All of these tasks are being done by machines. For example, 10-foot-high trees can be dug mechanically, and a large portion of their root systems are preserved. This could not have been done by hand. Some machines have been cleverly designed to dig large shade trees or evergreens and move them a few feet or many miles.

There are many types of facilities found at wholesale nurseries. Which ones you will need is determined by the requirements of the type of business you plan to operate. Many nurseries have greenhouses in which they propagate plants during winter using cuttings, grafts and even seeds. A comparatively recent introduction is a plastic-covered, round-topped structure used for summer softwood propagation and/or winter storage. They are called tunnel houses in England, a name that is appropriate.

Dormant deciduous stock ready for the market is usually dug in fall and stored in buildings especially constructed for that purpose. In these buildings, the temperature and moisture levels are regulated to keep the nursery stock in good condition over winter. Digging is done in fall so that grading can be done indoors during the winter months and shipments can be made when the customers want them.

"Grading" is one of the grower's most important functions. During the early days of the nursery industry — in fact, throughout most of the 19th century and the first quarter of the 20th — there was no universally accepted method or system of designating a plant's size or grade, let alone its quality. How many canes should a rosebush have to be No. 1? What should the diameter of a 10-foot-tall shade tree be? There are many other questions about sizes and quality. Retail nurserymen could never be sure of the grades they would receive when they placed their orders with the wholesale growers. If they inquired about the diameter of a typical 2-year-old apple tree, they might be told that it had about the same caliper as a broom stick, or a forefinger. Sizing was as indefinite as that.

The American Association of Nurserymen gave serious consideration to this problem at its very first meeting in 1876. A committee of the industry's leaders worked diligently on the problem. But the first standards were not published by that organization until almost 50 years later in 1923.

In the meantime, the Western, Oregon and Pacific Coast nurserymen associations had adopted grading standards for fruit trees, the most important class of nursery stock at that time. These standards had a marked influence on the industry. By the early 1900s, leading wholesale nurserymen had, on their own initiative, adopted more or less uniform standards for grading fruit trrees. These standards were generally accepted.

The first set of comprehensive grading standards for nursery stock was initially printed and approved by the American National Standards Institute (ANSI) in 1923. They have since been brought up to date from time to time. Today, these standards have made it possible for all members of the nursery trade in all parts of the country to trade with each other with a clear understanding of grades and quality.

For example, when retail nurserymen place orders for specific shade trees 10 feet high, they know what the maximum height, branching and caliper six inches above ground level should be. When they order rosebushes, No. 1 grade, they know the plants should have three or more strong stems, two of which will be 18 or more inches long.

It can be readily seen that these grading standards are of paramount importance to wholesale growers. They should be thoroughly familiar with them and apply them meticulously if they want to have and keep satisfied customers. By far the greater portion of nursery stock sold to consumers originates in wholesale nurseries. The wholesalers are responsible for grading the stock. They are the nurserymen who determine the grades, which had better be right. Their customers are familiar with these grades. Therefore, improper or careless grading only leads to trouble.

Grading standards have been developed for container-grown stock and are discussed in the chapter on container production.

Pricing

One of the most difficult tasks facing the wholesale grower is that of pricing. Theoretically, prices should be based on costs, but to apply costs to certain plants of definite grades is nearly impossible. If you grow only a very limited assortment of plants, you could come close in determining your cost per plant. However, when you grow a large assortment of plants that are 1-, 2- and 3-years-old or older, you care for all of them at the same time. The costs cannot be accurately assigned.

How then do you arrive at your prices? The price lists of nurserymen already established in the business reflect current wholesale prices. People beginning in the business need to be guided by these established rates if they want to be competitive. The current lists for fall or spring of any wholesale nursery represent the prices that the nurserymen believe are fair and will return reasonable profits. These prices were determined with the experiences of the previous year. If they thought that these prices would not generate enough profit, they might raise them, or vice versa.

There is one factor of pricing that you can determine accurately — the overall costs of doing business. This, of course, will be reflected in your prices. If your business fails to make a profit, your prices may be too low or your expenses too high, or both. This situation, of course, calls for either raising prices or cutting costs. Nurserymen usually raise their prices by adding a certain percentage to each class of plants. They rarely change the prices of individual varieties. Quite often, they raise prices across the board, affecting the entire range of plants. A wholesaler might announce that prices will increase 5 percent next season, across the board.

Prices are affected by competition. It might be necessary to reduce some prices to meet stiff competition. Oversupplies could call for some price reductions. However, a nursery that frequently cuts its prices is in danger of lowering its image. If a nursery consistently supplies good plants and renders good service, it will build a clientele of loyal customers willing to pay fair prices. All businesses have shoppers who constantly search for bargains, and the nursery business is no exception. Usually, such customers are hard to please and slow to pay.

A practice that has been followed in recent years by some wholesale nurserymen is that of giving discounts to some customers at the end of each season. The customers place their initial orders and then add to them as their needs arise. All of these orders are billed at regular prices. When the season ends and the customers pay all their bills, they receive their refunds. The specific percentage of the total bill refunded depends on the amount purchased. This practice encourages customers to buy as many of their needs as possible from one source and to pay their bills on time.

Not so long ago, wholesale nursery price lists were merely listings of varieties, sizes and prices. Sometimes, they included very boring descriptive notes. In other words, they contained the bare bones. Apparently, wholesalers assumed that retailers were well-informed and needed no help. Astute growers began to realize that retailers — many of whom were new in the business — did indeed need help in selecting the plants to buy. In fact, they needed to know a great deal about the plants being offered.

Growers began to include descriptions, illustrations and other helpful information. Today, the price lists of an increasing number of wholesalers are useful references. They include descriptions and full-color illustrations, which are, quite often, works of art.

Once you have grown, dug and graded your nursery stock, you must sell it. First, of course, come the price lists. You will then need a roster of retailers to whom you can send the price lists. You can best obtain this list by advertising in the trade press. There are several nursery trade journals. Together, they reach all parts of the country. All progressive retailers subscribe to them.

Nurseries advertising in these journals have to make what they are offering perfectly clear. Merely listing a name and address is not sufficient. Retailers scan these journals looking for specific items. They often place orders based on the advertisements they see. Retailers are always interested in something new; many of their customers are asking for something new or unusual. The best results are obtained from advertising year-round. The wholesaler's name then becomes familiar to the trade.

During the first 100 years of the nursery industry, most products were sold by salesmen who called on their prospects. This practice fulfilled the needs of the retail business, but no salesmen called on the retailers. A few wholesale salesmen began to appear on the scene during the first 25 years of this century, but it is doubtful if there were more than a dozen or two representing the large wholesale nurseries. These salesmen called on their employers' best customers.

Today, the wholesale salesman is the name of the game. Many hundreds represent the leading growers in the country and call on retail nurserymen in all corners of the nation. These salesmen are a boon to the industry.

Most are well-informed. Many work in nurseries and have first-hand knowledge of the plants, their uses and the nursery practices that produced them. Retailers do well to listen to these salesmen. While visiting garden centers, landscape nurserymen and other retailers, wholesale salesmen accumulate many valuable ideas for advertising, display merchandising, customer relations, management and other aspects of nursery operations. They can pass these ideas to their customers. They can also serve their employers by passing along to them customers' complaints, compliments and suggestions. Wholesalers are then in position to develop better relations with their custmers.

Despite the important roles wholesale salesmen play, the major portion of nursery stock sold at wholesale is proabably sold through the nurseries' catalogs and price lists. Only a small proportion of wholesale growers employ salesmen. The rest depend on price lists and advertisements to sell their products.

Now that you have sold the nursery stock, when and how will you deliver it? With some exceptions, most wholesale nurserymen do most of their shipping in spring. Often, certain plants do not mature early enough for fall digging. Also, early bad weather sometimes interferes. As we explained earlier, most nursery stock that is dug in fall is put into storage buildings where it can be graded nad readied for shipment. Retailers who have their own storage facilities like to get their stock in fall so that it can be ready for sale at the proper time in spring.

Spring Rush

The busiest time for the entire nursery industry is spring. That is when most people do their planting, and the season for planting is comparatively short. As we have already indicated, some retailers have storage facilities and can have their nursery stock shipped in fall so that it is ready as soon as spring arrives. Those retailers who depend on spring delivery, however, naturally want their plants as soon as the planting season opens.

This puts tremendous pressure on wholesale nurserymen. Only a few wholesalers have their own trucks for making deliveries; most depend on contract truck haulers, who are not always available at the right time. Some will travel only to limited areas, while others are not reliable. Some retailers call for their orders with their own trucks. The spring shipping season is a trying time, but the job always gets done.

Wholesale nurserymen, as a rule, do not guarantee delivery of orders in good condition because they have no control over the shipments once they leave their hands. Shipments travel at the risk and expense of the customers. Claims for damage to plants should be made to the carriers. Neither do wholesalers guarantee that their plants will grow. Memorandums, published by the wholesalers in their price lists, are known as non-warranties. A typical example is, "We give no warranty, expressed or implied, as to the life, description, quality, productiveness or any other matter of any stock that we sell, and will not in any way be responsible for the results secured in transplanting."

Instructions to the customers then follow: "Claims for any cause must be made promptly upon receipt of goods. We will not entertain claims after goods have been accepted, or when report is not made in writing within 10 days after arrival of stock."

The basis for these conditions is the assumption that the customers, retail nurserymen, understand the grading standards for nursery stock and are qualified to judge the condition of the shipments when they arrive. If they are not qualified, they are not capable of judging the conditions of the stock. That should not be the responsibility of the wholesaler.

All states, with a few possible exceptions, require that nurseries be licensed. Furthermore, nurseries are subject to annual or semiannual inspections to make sure that their stock is free of injurious insects and diseases. Nurseries found free of these pests are issued a certificate of inspection. Copies of this certificate must accompany all shipments of nursery stock.

In recent years, a new type of wholesale nurseryman has appeard. The best name that we can apply to them is "Jobber," although they may use the word "nursery" in the "names" of their businesses. Jobbers grow no nursery stock, but buy it and make it available to retail nursery operations, such as

WHOLESALE NURSERIES

garden centers and landscape nurserymen. They can operate successfully only in the vicinity of big cities, where there are many retail nursery outlets.

During the planting season, jobbers carry a well-balanced assortment of trees, shrubs, evergreens and so on. Bare-root plants, including such items as flowering shrubs, hedge plants, fruit trees, small shade trees, rosebushes and so on, are held in storage buildings where they are kept dormant and viable. Outdoors under overhead shade, the jobbers keep larger plants, such as large evergreens and shade trees, as well as a balanced assortment of container-grown plants. They offer a valuable service to retail nurserymen, who can quickly obtain the plants they need in all sorts of emergencies. Understandably, the jobbers' prices are higher than those of the wholesale growers. Usually, they make no deliveries, but serve call-in trade.

Chapter 9. Financing and Records

Financing and Records

When anyone starts a nursery business — or any other business — the matter of finances must receive careful consideration. Indeed, finances are of paramount importance. Year after year, Dun & Bradstreet Credit Services, the giant, credit-reporting company, has reported that the chief cause of business failure is lack of adequate capital and poor business management.

Unless beginners in the nursery business already have adequate financial resources to become established, they have to borrow money. The logical source, of course, is a bank. Whether they can borrow is, of course, a matter entirely between them and their bankers. Bankers will ask the applicants many questions that, we hope, they will be able to answer after reading this book.

A little-known source of help in establishing a business or profession is the Small Business Administration, which is a federal agency. It was set up specifically to provide financial help to people beginning a small business or a profession. It has offices in many cities and has aided thousands of individuals. Your banker can give you the address of the nearest office.

There are nurserymen in business today who, unable to finance full-scale operations, began their businesses as sidelines while they held other jobs. This gave them security and relieved some of the worries associated with starting a business. We recommend this plan to people who have limited financial resources. It takes longer, but it may be the only way for many people to establish their businesses.

It is likely that a simple landscape business has the greatest advantage. You can begin this type of business with the least amount of capital if you are prepared to do most of the work yourself at the outset. Assuming you are qualified to do landscape designing and planting and have some ability as a salesman, you can start your business with only enough capital to buy the nursery stock you need to plant your first few jobs. With the money you make on these jobs, you can purchase the stock for your next jobs. And you can operate your business from your home. Some fairly large landscape businesses are run entirely from the owners' homes.

One good example comes to mind. In a suburb of a large Midwestern city, a young man started a small nursery business some years ago while he worked in the city as a bank clerk. Most of his business was run from his backyard. His business, consisting mostly of small landscape jobs and cash-and-carry sales, was conducted on evenings and holidays. At first, he bought all the stock he needed. Later, he started growing some stock on a nearby tract of land.

After a few years, his business had increased to such an extent that he felt safe in leaving his bank job and devoting his full time to the nursery business. The stock he had produced in the intervening years made it unnecessary to buy more. He then used more of his capital to expand his grounds and equipment. Today, his operation is one of the most progressive and successful nurseries in the area.

In another city, not far away, is a highly successful nursery business that began in a similar fashion. An accountant for a large publishing house wanted to increase his income. He had always been interested in plants and especially in roses, which he cultivated with better than average success. His neighbors and friends wanted some of the ones he had produced. He made a deal with the nursery from which he bought his stock to pay him a small commission on the sales he made.

He soon found that he could make more profit by buying the roses outright at wholesale prices and reselling them at retail. Before long, his backyard was too small to hold all the nursery stock he needed for his business, which he conducted in his spare time. He bought a plot of ground in a suburban area and borrowed money to build a combination home, office, storage and sales building. His wife looked after the rapidly growing business while he continued to work as an accountant.

They established their business in a city where there happened to be little competition. The demand for landscape services grew so much that they opened a landscape division in addition to their cash-and-carry operation. Their volume of business was finally so great that the accountant resigned and became a full-time, prosperous nurseryman.

Budgeting

Once you are established in business, one of the most important next steps is to make a budget and use it. It is surprising how many small businesses operate without budgets. In the simplest terms, a budget is a list of the amounts of money that will be needed during the ensuing year for all facets of the business, including wages, rent, utilities, insurance, interest, merchandise, repairs and so on. The actual list depends entirely on the nature of the business. Studying this budget may reveal ways to save money.

A budget shows how much money will be needed to operate the business for the coming fiscal year. The nursery business, being seasonal, has some inherent low-income periods, when it is necessary to borrow money. Since the slack periods are well-known, nurserymen can forecast quite closely the times when they will have to borrow.

Because your budget indicates how much money you will need, you can design a sales program that will generate enough income to cover all your expenses and leave a profit. The longer a business is operated on a budget, the more helpful it becomes in promoting good management.

In the nursery business, inventory turnover is comparatively slow. Even under ideal conditions, you cannot hope to turn your stock over more than $1\frac{1}{2}$ or 2 times a year. To do this, you have to buy all your stock and be where your climate permits you to plant practically all year.

In most of the US, there is limited planting in fall. The main planting season comes only once a year, in spring. It is likely that the average turnover in the nursery business is only once in 2 or 3 years. Some nursery stock can be produced in one growing season, but most of it takes 2 or more years to reach marketable sizes.

Contrast this with the food business. Bakery goods, for example, turn over practically every day, fresh fruits and meats do so every few days. It is probably true that a food store's entire stock turns over an average of once a month, or a dozen times a year. Of course, food products are sold at a very low markup, making rapid turnover a necessity. Even retail florists who buy all of their flowers might turn their stocks over every few days. Obviously, a business that enjoys a rapid turnover can operate on less capital.

As we mentioned before, beginners in the nursery business tend to price their stocks too low. You can readily see that, as a nurseryman, you cannot operate on a margin as small as that of a food market. Even if your turnover rate were once a year, you would have to make a profit of 24¢ on the dollar to realize the same return as the food market does with a profit of 2¢.

There are also other factors to consider when pricing stock. Nursery products are perishable; some will die before it is sold. The items that remain unsold at the end of the season may become liabilities unless they can be carried into the next season in good salable condition. You may have to replace some of the stock you sold to customers. You must also consider the expense of getting stock from the grower to your nursery and the expense of handling and displaying the plants after they arrive.

How to Figure Markup

To better understand the problem of pricing nursery stock, you should be familiar with the process of figuring markups. Simply, a markup is the difference between an item's cost and its selling price. If a product costs 50¢ and sells for $1, the markup is 50¢. However, markups are usually expressed as percentages.

Many nurserymen, particularly those new in the business, are in the habit of figuring the percentage of markup based on cost. In our example, the selling price is double the cost. The percentage of markup based on cost is 100 percent. But this way of figuring the percentage of markup has long since been discarded by retailers.

Instead, retailers now base the percentage on the item's selling price. To do this, subtract the cost from the selling price and divide the difference by the selling price. Again using our exmple, a 50¢ cost subtracted from a selling price of $1 leaves 50¢. Dividing 50¢ by the selling price, $1, produces a markup of 50 percent.

With this method, it is impossible to mark up an item 100 percent. For example, your retail price on a certain item is $5, five times that of its cost, $1. Your markup ($5 − $1, or $4, divided by $5) is 80 percent. One of the chief advantages of this system is to help merchants avoid underpricing their merchandise. It makes them realize that their markups may not be as large as they might at first appear to be.

There is no infallible formula that you can follow in pricing nursery stock. In general, the higher the cost, the lower the markup should be. For example, a shrub costing $1 might retail readily for $3, a markup of 66⅔ percent, but an evergreen costing $25 might not retail for more than $50 or $60, a markup of 50 or 58 percent. You do not need such a high percentage of markup on the higher priced items, because your dollar profit per unit of sale is much greater.

Bank Credit

No matter how you finance your business, you should try to establish bank credit. At one time or another, most businesses find it mecessary to borrow money to tide them over periods of heavy expense or low income, especially if they want to finance expansion programs. If your banker wants a list of your assets and a statement of your business prospects when you apply for a loan, do not consider it an affront, but give them to him freely. He needs that information before he can make an intelligent decision on your application.

You will find it very convenient to be able to buy from your wholesale sources on open account. In this way, you do not need to bother figuring out the amount of the order or to send a check. If you pay in advance and the order is not filled completely, as often happens, you have to wait for your refund, and your bookkeeping is complicated. When applying for credit from wholesalers, give them the names of other companies from which you have been buying on credit, and supply any other pertinent information they need to decide if you are entitled to an open account.

After you have established your trade credit, guard it jealously. Never permit your obligations to become so large that you cannot take care of them readily. Pay all your bills promptly, even before they are due, especially if a discount is offered. Receiving discounts for early payments is not only an easy way to make money, but it gives you a

FINANCING AND RECORDS

higher credit rating. Someone has wisely said that next to your bank account, your credit is your best asset.

Wholesalers' Discounts

Some wholesale nurseries offer a discount for paying in advance of shipment. If the discount is greater than that allowed under the regular open account terms, it might be good business to make the advance payments. In general, it is advisable to take advantage of any discounts that are offered. They represent good returns on your investment. Suppose you buy $500 worth of nursery stock on open account with terms of 2 percent 10 days, net 30 days from date of invoice. You could let the account run the full 30 days, but if you paid in 10 days, you would earn the 2 percent discount, or $10.

There are approximately 12 30-day periods in a year; so your discount represents an earning at the annual rate of 24 percent. If you are offered a 3 percent discount for payment in advance of shipment, your earning rate would be 36 percent. It would be hard to beat that kind of rate in the nursery business.

Do not expect a wholesaler to finance your business. When you permit an invoice to run past a due date, you are, in effect, forcing the wholesaler to act as your banker. Many businessmen fail to understand this. When they withhold money that is due, they are using money that belongs to the wholesalers, who may have to borrow money to cover periods of lean income. This means that the wholesalers are paying interest to carry the delinquent accounts.

This is not good business for the wholesalers because the interest they are paying comes out of their profits. And it is not good business for delinquent dealers. The wholesalers will hesitate to give them credit again, and the dealers may have difficulty gretting credit from other wholesalers because businessmen often exchange credit information. Always bear in mind that good credit is one of your most valuable assets.

Bank Loans

If you should find yourself unable to pay an account when it is due, you should try to borrow the money you need from a bank. Loaning money is the bank's business. This is one reason why you should establish bank credit. Another is that wholesalers often charge interest on past-due accounts. The rate varies a great deal but is usually higher than the rate a bank charges. For this reason alone, it is good business to borrow money, if it is necessary, to pay your bills.

However, if you cannot borrow the money, your next best alternative is to lay your cards on the table with the wholesaler. Explain your situation: why you are unable to pay now and — as nearly as you can — when you will be able to pay. It is always better to make partial payments from time to time to show your good intentions than to wait until you are able to pay the entire amount that is due.

Once you have made your position clear to the wholesalers, you will find that most of them will do all they can to go along with you until you are able to pay them. They are interested in keeping you, not only as a customer but also as a solvent customer.

Chapter 10. Miscellany

Miscellany

Nursery Associations

The nursery industry is highly organized. Almost every state has a nurserymen's association. There are also several regional associations, the oldest of which is the Western Association of Nurserymen. It was established in 1890, and its headquarters are in Kansas City, KS. Nurserymen in each type of nursery business have banded together to form associations with national memberships.

Topping them all is the national association, the American Association of Nurserymen (AAN). Organized in 1876, the AAN has experienced a healthy growth ever since. The membership, drawn from the US and Canada, numbers several thousand.

Of the multitudes of national business associations with headquarters in Washington, DC, the AAN is one of the most active, effective and respected in serving its membership.

The staff of the AAN administers the activities of five allied industry groups: Garden Centers of America Inc., Horticultural Research Institute Inc., National Association of Plant Patent Owners Inc., National Landscape Association Inc. and Wholesale Nursery Growers of America Inc.

An active national organization that does not come under the aegis of the AAN is the Mailorder Association of Nurserymen.

The AAN is fully aware that one of the greatest needs of the nursery industry is better management skills. To remedy this condition, it sponsors several educational seminars in various parts of the country every year. These have been well-attended and have proved a great boon to the industry.

The AAN keeps a watchful eye on Federal Legislation, proposals and enactments that may affect the nursery industry. It offers, at considerable savings, group insurance in several categories. It promotes national radio advertising to stimulate interest in planting. This is financed by voluntary contributions of the industry members. The AAN provides many other services. All nurserymen should be members of the AAN as well as of their state associations.

Professionalism

A great deal has been said and written about professionalism in the nursery business, and especially about the lack of it and the need for more. There are differing concepts of what this term entails. This, however, is what professionalism usually means when applied to the nursery business: To be a professional, a nurseryman must be thoroughly informed about the business, its requirements, obligations and products. This may not conform to the dictionary's definition, but it is appropriate to the nursery business. Of course, the nursery business is not a profession in the strictest sense of the word.

It is not an uncommon practice for garden center operators to boast of their professionalism. They encourage home gardeners to come to them for help with their problems, saying "We are professionals; let us help you." There are numerous garden centers that qualify for this label by having professional personnel. The owners and employees are well-informed about the qualities and requirements of the plants they sell.

Unfortunately, an acceptable degree of professionalism is lacking in many garden centers, even in some that claim to possess it. Recognizing this fact, nursery associations in several states have designed study courses for employees — and owners — of garden centers. If followed conscientiously, these courses could qualify employees as professionals. In these state programs, examinations were given to learn if the students qualified. Interestingly, a number of garden center owners and managers failed. The program was very successful but, unfortunately, it has not proliferated.

Some progressive garden center owners encourage employees who lack horticultural knowledge to learn by offering bonuses as incentives. They also give guidance to make the studies worthwhile. It is not always possible for garden centers to employ people who are already professional, so the problem remains, awaiting solution.

Trade Shows

During the past few years, something new has occurred in the nursery industry — trade shows. Most are held in connection with association conventions. The shows began as modest and small events. A nurseryman would bring a few specimen plants to a convention and find a place to exhibit them, usually in the convention hotel's lobby. Sometimes a distributor of products used by nurserymen would exhibit some wares. At that time, no provision was made for exhibits.

The practice, however, gained acceptance and grew until the number of the exhibits necessitated arrangements for exhibit space. A separate room in the hotel was set aside for them. Some shows had so many exhibits that the association members did not have time to visit all of them without missing some of the convention sessions. Eventually, certain hours were set aside for the specific purpose of visiting the exhibits.

Some association conventions attract hundreds of exhibitors. There are regional conventions that draw thousands of visitors.

The shows do not consist only of exhibits by nurserymen. Many manufacturers and distributors of products used by nurserymen and sold in their garden shops are there. These trade shows serve a very useful purpose for nurserymen. Many retailers place orders for the coming season with exhibitors.

There is no shortage of trade shows. Nearly every state association, however small, believes it is obligatory to stage a trade show in connection with its annual convention. There are so many shows held in so many parts of the country that no nurseryman needs to travel far to attend one.

Mass-Market Competition

Mass marketers are in the nursery business; some of them have been for many years. When they entered this area of merchandising, they wanted plants they could sell at low prices. And that is what they got — small, root-wrapped plants of inferior quality and poorly packaged. Not only was the plants' quality poor, but the stores offered no services at all. There was no one around to provide customers with the information they most needed.

Over the years, this situation has changed. The quality of the plants offered by mass marketers is now generally quite good, and their packaging has improved markedly. However, they still offer no services. No one is available to give customers advice. Plants are often poorly displayed and not properly cared for. Mass marketers often leave plants in poor condition on sale, and, at times, offer plants that are not adapted to the area.

Some garden center owners are fearful of this mass-market competition. It is not going to go away. The sale of nursery stock must earn enough profit to be interesting or the stores would have given it up long ago. But there is little reason for garden center owners to worry about mass-market competition.

First of all, you should remember that most mass marketers have nursery stock on sale only a few weeks in spring and rarely in fall. Their assortments are limited, and their prices do not represent bargains. Not many customers go to mass markets to buy plants. Rather, they see them when they visit the stores. Customer purchases are mostly impulse ones.

The gardeners who take pride in their home grounds are not mass marketer customers. They are interested in the best material. They do not want to make any mistakes while planting. They go to garden centers where they can get professional help — and information on which they can rely. Garden centers that offer a broad selection of good plants adapted to the area and provide courteous and dependable service will be able to meet the challenge of mass-market competition.

Plant Patents

Many years ago, the US patent laws were amended to make it possible to patent plants. This was promoted by nurserymen against much opposition, even by other nurserymen, who felt that all plants should be available to all people without restriction.

To be patented, a plant has to be entirely new. Such plants come about through hybridization or natural cloning ("sporting," as it is often called). A patent gives the owner exclusive rights to the propagation and sale of the new plant. Many thousands of plants have been patented through the years. Some lawyers make careers by helping clients get plant patents.

To make any money from these new plants, it is necessary, of course, to propagate and sell them. A few patent owners do both, retaining all rights for themselves. However, the more common practice is to license other nurserymen to grow and sell the plants. These nurserymen pay the patent owners royalties on all the plants they produce. Roses are among the most widely distributed patented plants.

Guarantees

Guaranteeing wholesale stock has already been discussed. However, retail material is different. Most retail customers probably want to know if the plants they are buying carry any sort of guarantee or warranty. No doubt most garden center operators offer some sort of guarantee or warranty. However, some do not.

One highly successful garden center owner in a small, Midwestern town offers no guarantee at all. He does not publicize the fact but, if asked what guarantee he offers, he replies "Those plants are guaranteed until you go out the gate with them. They are alive and thriving now. The rest is up to you." Not many nurserymen could get away with that, but in his case, he and most of his customers are friends. His customers know that he will treat them fairly. But in most cases, customers want some assurance that the plants they buy will give them good results. If the plants fail, the customers want recourse.

Nursery stock guarantees come in many styles. Some nurseries refund the purchase price if a plant fails to grow by a certain date and is returned with the sales slip. Others make the same offer but do not require the plants be returned. Some nurseries replace plants if they fail to survive until a certain date, often several months after their purchase. And some garden centers offer unconditional guarantees: If a plant does not survive the first growing season, the customer's money is refunded. This, by the way, is a rather common practice of mass marketers.

In communities with several garden centers, the owners often get together and agree on a uniform guarantee to be observed by all. It could be a policy of non-warranty. The guarantee is posted in each establishment. Sometimes these guarantees are so restrictive that customers are antagonized. Therefore, many garden centers have definitive policies but do not publish them.

More and more garden centers are not establishing any sort of guarantee at all. They handle each case on its own merits, which usually means that the first objective is to satisfy the customer. One way of doing this is to tell the customers of your interest in satisfying them.

If they do not voluntarily tell you what they want as compensation, you can say, "We want you to be satisified. Please tell us what you think would be a fair adjustment." This often takes the steam out of the customers' dissatisfation, and their requests are usually very reasonable. Many garden centers have found that the adjustment costs are moderate and are more than offset by keeping the customers happy. Otherwise they might be lost.

Computers

Do nurserymen use computers? The answer is yes. A few have used them for a long time, and now computers are being used by hundreds of nurserymen. The problem at first was to get the machines programmed specifically for nurserymen. Proper software is now available.

There are many ways that computers can be helpful to nurserymen. One of the most useful functions for wholesale nurserymen is that of inventory control. Wholesalers must maintain accurate records of what they have available for sale, and that information must be available with little delay.

For example, assume that a customer phones in wanting 100 sugar maple trees 8 to 10 feet tall. Does the wholesaler have them? The customer needs to know right then. There are manual systems that accomplish this, but the computer can do it much more rapidly. Such information provided in this fashion helps nurserymen avoid overselling.

Computers can serve nurserymen in many other ways. Among them are invoicing, payroll, customer files, addressing catalogs, order booking, accounts receivable and payable, and so on.

Remember that the computer is only an electronic mechanical device. It cannot think. The information that it spews forth is based upon the information fed into it. If this information is erroneous, the computer's answers will be incorrect. Nwevertheless, a computer can be a very valuable asset.

Trade Journals

In the US, there are several national nursery trade journals. They render a very valuable service to the industry.

If you are looking for a certain variety of plant, you are likely to find it in a trade journal advertisement. Hundreds of growers advertise their stock in these journals. New introductions, as well as rare plants, are offered.

All sorts of standard equipment and new products nurserymen need in the field, storage house, office and greenhouse are also advertised. The journals report on conventions and meetings that have been held or will be held. News of the industry, businesses and personnel are duly noted. From these journals, you can learn of new regulations that affect the industry. Qualified people write articles of interest and importance to nurserymen. Trade journals offer many amenities. The nurserymen who believe they can keep up with the industry without reading the trade journals are deceiving themselves.

The Future

The prospects for success for people who enter the nursery business during the present era are indeed good. Important developments during the past few decades have raised both production and marketing practices to their highest levels of efficiency.

The garden center, which came into being after World War II, has been a great boon to the industry. At the garden center, customers can get the information and advice they need. Close relationships between nurserymen and customers can develop and are beneficial to both. The importance of this becomes evident when one realizes that gardening is near the top of the list of hobbies among Americans.

The landscape branch of the nursery business is flourishing, both as an independent operation and as part of the garden center business. Homes are no longer thought of as complete until they are landscaped.

The introduction of container-grown plants has brought great and beneficial changes to the industry — almost a revolution. The planting season has been greatly extended. Dormant bare-root plants can be safely planted only during comparatively brief periods in spring and autumn. Container-grown plants can be set out almost any time — year-round in many parts of the country. The survival rate of container-grown plants is consistently better than that of dormant plants. This produces happier customers.

The nursery industry offers inviting opportunities for developing thriving businesses.